Bridgin ministry today

Edited by Gordon W. Kuhrt and Pat Nappin

CHURCH HOUSE PUBLISHING

Church House Publishing
Church House
Great Smith Street
London SW1P 3NZ

ISBN 0 7151 2607 5

Published 2002 by Church House Publishing

Acknowledgements
Scripture quotations are taken from *The New Revised Standard Version of
the Bible* © 1989 The Division of Christian Education of the National
Council of Churches in the USA.

Extract from *The Canons of the Church of England*, 6th edn, Church House
Publishing, 2000 are copyright © The Archbishops' Council, 2000.

Typeset in Rotis by Vitaset, Paddock Wood, Kent

Printed by Creative Print and Design Group, Ebbw Vale, Wales

Contents

Notes on contributors

Canon Dr Christina Baxter
Christina has been Principal of St John's College, Nottingham, since 1997. She joined the staff there in 1979 after seven years teaching in a sixth form college, followed by a Durham Research Studentship which enabled her to write a thesis on Karl Barth's theological method. She is Chairman of the General Synod's House of Laity in the Church of England, in which capacity she serves on several national committees. She is a Reader in the rural parishes of Awsworth and Cossall in Southwell Diocese, and an Honorary Canon Theologian at Coventry Cathedral and Canon at Southwell Minster. She enjoys preaching and teaching, whether it is at large conferences or in the parish room with a handful of teenagers. She takes a keen interest in women's issues. In her spare time, Christina enjoys swimming, theatre, music, entertaining, gardening and all things creative.

Canon Pat Nappin
Pat has been a Reader for 28 years. In retirement she became Deputy Honorary Secretary of the Central Readers' Council in 1997 and Honorary Secretary in 1999. Her career was in education and she taught in Birmingham, Bath, California and Barking before becoming Head of three schools, all in the London Borough of Barking and Dagenham. She represented the Diocese of Chelmsford on the General Synod from 1975 to 2000 and served two terms on the panel of Chairmen. She was made a Lay Canon of Chelmsford Cathedral in January 2000. In her spare time she enjoys music, the theatre, eating out and especially travel.

Mr Andrew Britton
Andrew Britton is a Reader at St Margaret's, Chipstead in Surrey. He worked as an economist at the Treasury, and then as director of the National Institute of Economic and Social Research. He was also one of the Chancellor's independent advisors – the so-called 'wise men'. After that he worked full-time for two years as executive secretary of the Churches' Enquiry into Unemployment and the Future of Work, sponsored by the Council of Churches for Britain and Ireland. He is now chairman of the Southwark Diocesan Board of Finance and also a member of DRACSC, the committee of the Archbishops' Council concerned with deployment, remuneration and conditions of service for clergy and others in ministry.

Mrs Margaret Hounsham
Margaret Hounsham was licensed as a Reader in the Diocese of Portsmouth ten years ago. She is currently the Reader of the parish of St Philip, Cosham. She works for the Diocese of Winchester as a Lay Training Officer enabling lay people to take an active part in parish life and coordinating Reader training. At present she is working on a dissertation to complete a Master of Theology in Preaching with the College of Preachers and Spurgeon's College. She is married to Alan, a civil engineer, and they have two children in their late teens.

Mrs Wendy Thorpe
Wendy Thorpe is married to a Reader and has two sons and grandchildren. Her career in teaching and training has been varied, including three years in the Philippines as executive director of Headstart Inc. and 10 years as principal of an adult education centre in Gosport. She became Reader in Portsmouth diocese in 1986, first in St Mary's, Alverstoke, then in St Peter's, Bishop's Waltham. Her main ministry interests are Reader training, training the laity for leadership, Alpha and the ministry of healing prayer. She was director of Reader training for Portsmouth Diocese for four years before taking up her present appointment as national moderator for Reader training. She has an office in the Ministry Division at Church House, Westminster but spends most of her time travelling the country to conferences and regional meetings of moderators and presenting moderation reports to diocesan bishops.

Mrs Caroline Pascoe
Caroline Pascoe is a Reader in Gloucester Diocese. She has ministered in town, city, suburban and rural communities and taught in secondary comprehensive schools. She is currently principal of the Gloucester Local Ministry and Ordained Local Ministry Scheme. She is a director of the Edward King Institute for Ministry Development and a member of the Ministry Division's Deployment, Remuneration and Conditions of Service Committee and its Continuing Ministerial Education Panel. Her first book, *The Ministry Team Handbook II*, will be published by SPCK later in 2002.

Venerable Dr Gordon Kuhrt
Gordon Kuhrt was a Reader when a schoolteacher. Following ordination he has been a tutor and Warden for Readers in the Dioceses of Lichfield, Canterbury and Southwark. After over twenty years of parish ministry he was Archdeacon of Lewisham 1989–1996 and was then appointed as Head of Department of the then Advisory Board for Ministry, which has now become the Ministry Division. He has published several books, including *Believing in Baptism, An Introduction to Christian Ministry* (CHP 2000) and, most recently, *Ministry Issues for the Church of England* (CHP, 2001). His wife is a Reader.

Foreword

What is a Reader – what does it mean – how does it work out in practice? These and others are questions addressed in this book. Incredibly this is the first introductory book written since women were admitted as Readers in 1969. Much has changed since that time, with Readers and other lay ministers playing an increasingly significant part in the ministry of the Church. The book is much needed to fill a gap in the information available to Christians trying to discover their vocation.

The Church of the twenty-first century needs to recognize the contribution of all people in ministry. Here is a trained, authorized ministry freely given in order that the message of the gospel can be better understood and people helped and encouraged by those who live and work alongside them. To be a Reader is challenging, exciting and immensely rewarding, as readers of this book will discover. Over ten thousand people from all walks of life have found this for themselves. Perhaps God is calling you to join them; read on and pray that he will speak to you in these chapters.

✠ Graham Dow
Bishop of Carlisle
Chair of the Central Readers' Council

Chapter 1

Good stewards of the manifold grace of God

Christina Baxter

The end of all things is near; therefore be serious and discipline yourselves for the sake of your prayers. Above all, maintain constant love for one another for love covers a multitude of sins. Be hospitable to one another, without complaining. Like good stewards of the manifold grace of God, serve one another with whatever gift each of you has received. Whoever speaks must do so as one speaking the very words of God; whoever serves must do so with the strength that God supplies, so that God may be glorified in all things through Jesus Christ. To him belong the glory and the power for ever and ever. Amen. (1 Peter 4.7-11)

What is a Reader?

I began to exercise the ministry of Reader about thirty years ago, although at the time I had little theological understanding of what I was embarking upon. Through the last few months, I have been thinking particularly about 1 Peter 4.7-11 (quoted above) which has increasingly seemed to me to sum up what might be said of a Reader (though I am not suggesting that that was what Peter had in mind as he wrote!). I hope that my reflections may provide some guidance to all the ten thousand and more Readers in the Church of England who typically get on with the things that need to be done rather than develop complex theories of what they are. The lack of simple definition is a Godsend; we can be as flexible as we need to be, within the frame-work of the Canons of the Church of England (see the Appendix, page 63), which enables us to fit exactly the many different situations in which we are placed.

1

Any understanding of ministry today in the Church of England begins with the theology of 'gracious gift' which stood at the head of the thinking in the Turnbull report.[1] This affirmed to us that God does not withhold from his Church all that is necessary for the Church to obey him. Readers have been part of God's good gift to the Church, in order that his people may worship, learn, receive pastoral ministry, obey God and continue in his mission. Readers are not an essential part of God's ministerial provision; other times and other places may not have Readers, but they have been one of the lay ministries which God has used to grow his Church in this part of the world in modern times.

We also set our understanding within the framework of a trinitarian theology which recognizes that the unity of God is a call to the Church to be united, and the differentiation of Father, Son and Holy Spirit within the Godhead encourages us to see that there can be genuine difference of gifting and tasks which does not destroy unity but enriches and contributes to it. Readers play their part in the manifold patterns of ministry which have been developing throughout the Church's history, but perhaps in new ways in the last 150 years or so, showing by virtue of their call and commission that ministry is always properly plural (Readers are always assistant ministers) and mutual (Readers both receive and give ministry).

Nothing in the vision I have sketched so far means that Readers have always been perfect or that they have always been welcomed by others who exercise the ordained oversight ministry as priests/presbyters and bishops in the Church. Bad experiences on either side need repentance and restoration/renewal. God's forgiving love covers a multitude of sins (verse 8) as does our forgiving love for one another. Only a fresh start will enable the Church to receive the fullness of God's gifts to the Church which many different kinds of ministry represent.

I realize of course, that in two ways I am adapting these verses from 1 Peter: first they were written to all Christians and not just to a particular group; second they are admonitions as to how to live, whereas I am taking them as characteristics of how Readers do live. I do not make apology for this since Readers are Christians – we are no more than that. Readers are usually mature Christians whom one should not be surprised to find have taken these admonitions to heart, and therefore are living them out in their daily lives. Indeed if this were not the case, they probably would not have been asked to become Readers in the first place. Readers are Christians in whom the manifold grace of God is at work, and who rejoice in being collaborators with God in this process.

The bigger picture

The perspective of our ministry – eschatology: God's timing

The end of all things is near. (verse 7)

With all the Church of God, Readers recognize that we live in the end times, which gives a sense of urgency to all that we do. Since the first coming of Jesus, Christians have been expecting his return, and in the light of his nearness, kingdom values and priorities are appropriate and these do not coincide with those of the world around. This world is not our home, in the words of a famous spiritual, 'we are just a-passing through', so this is not the time for building grand schemes or establishing permanent and inflexible patterns of ministry.

Readers should have a sense of the urgency of the kingdom of God. As lay people, who spend most of their time in the world, they know very well the need for kingdom values in their places of work and their homes, and the homes of their neighbours. If they did not have this conviction, they would not give themselves to a period of training and to regular ministry not only in their home church, but increasingly, with dioceses asking them to be 'deployable', travelling to other churches to enable the worship and teaching of fellow Christians in other congregations.

Perhaps there is a special ministry for Readers at the beginning of the twenty-first century, in their consciousness of the way in which God's kingdom values differ from everyday life. It is undoubtedly true that the Church of England's mission is hindered because most lay people do not understand the urgent need to give five per cent of their take home pay to the Church, allowing their other giving to go to other charitable work. In the area of allowing God's values to prevail, money is one of the most difficult, and yet many congregations are inclined to think when the priest speaks of these matters, they are either appealing for their own stipend, or they are bound to speak like that since they are professionals. An army of over ten thousand Readers who take a lead in preaching and teaching on those passages of Scripture which deal with giving, and who themselves are practising sacrificial giving would turn round the scandal of the Church's impoverishment and incapacity to do the work God is calling it to do, for instance, among young people. A sense of the nearness of the end enables us to be free from the world's insistence that we live as though we are eternal, and the expectation that the current world order of increased standards and luxury is here to stay.

The purpose of our ministry – the glory of God

> So that God may be glorified in all things through Jesus Christ. To him
> belong the glory and the power forever and ever. Amen. (verse 11)

There can be no other purpose for any Christian ministry, which is why it is
so important to make that very plain when we describe Readers. Why do we
visit the sick, take services, lead Bible study groups, preach sermons, or a
thousand and one other things? Put simply, we do these things so that God
may be glorified in our lives, in the lives of those we serve and in God's world
for which we care.

Like every other public ministry, as Readers we are constantly in danger of
thinking more highly of ourselves than we ought. Robes, and sitting at the
'sharp end' of church sometimes trip us up. How do we avoid that danger?
First by reminding ourselves of the one to whom all glory (if there is such a
thing in or from our ministries) belongs – God. Second, recognizing that
stewards have things entrusted to them, but those things are never owned by
the stewards, who may be asked to give up what has been entrusted to them
at any time.

A few years ago I attended the funeral of a Reader who had taught me religious
education at school. In retirement she had ministered in a country parish and
been very self-doubting about what she did and how she did it. I knew hardly
anyone at the funeral which was in a church packed to overflowing, but I spoke
to many people whose faith had been enlivened, strengthened and stretched
by this Reader's ministry. It was wonderfully inspiring and left me more aware
of the glory of God than of my sorrow. Once again I was aware of the economy
of God who uses very frail or apparently insignificant things – seeds – to bring
about a phenomenal harvest. Our being clay pots (see 2 Corinthians 4.7) only
serves to highlight the glory of God whose glory we serve.

The wellspring of our ministry – the grace of God

> Stewards of the manifold grace of God. (verse 10)

Peter refers to the abundance of the grace of the trinitarian God at the very
beginning of his letter (1 Peter 1.2), encouraging his readers to 'set all your
hope on the grace which Jesus Christ will bring you when he is revealed' (1.13).
It is a theme with which he closes his letter too: 'after you have suffered for
a little while, the God of all grace, who has called you to his eternal glory in
Christ, will himself restore, strengthen and establish you' (5.10). As God's grace
is inexhaustible, so too it is given in many different ways. Those who minister
do not offer themselves, but they offer to others the grace of God. Like aid
workers distributing food which others have donated, Christian ministers are

simply 'stewards of God's grace' which will never run out even when the steward tires or wears out. The grace of God may take forms in those to whom it is offered which we do not experience ourselves. Over twenty years ago I spoke to a small group of people at the church where I worship and found when I returned three months later (after an overseas trip) that they had received, as a result of God speaking through what I said that night, the gift of tongues – which gift I had not at that time been given. When I discovered what had happened I felt as if I had planted an apple pip and an orange tree had grown! But this passage has helped me to see that God had given his grace to me in one way, but he gave his manifold grace to my hearers in other ways – appropriate for them. It is so easy to think that the purpose of ministry is to make others like us, instead of enabling them to be open to God so that he can do in them what will bless them and glorify God.

If we are to be stewards of God's manifold grace that means that we need to be constantly open to receive it – as God gives to us different gifts and fruits in varied ways through our lives. Constant outpouring or passing on, which is what this stewarding suggests, means that there needs to be constant filling and reliance on God.

Readers know that they have received of the manifold grace of God, which they do not possess but simply manage, administer or steward for others.

The inner picture

Reader ministry is the ministry of openness. Few people 'promote themselves' into being Readers. Most respond to the suggestion of others, or the requests of ordained ministers to be open to this kind of service. This kind of openness is a major feature of the 'inner picture' – open to God in prayer and open to other people in love and hospitality, these are the characteristics which our text suggests that we might find in Readers.

Disciplined people who pray

> Therefore be serious and discipline yourselves for the sake of your prayer. (verse 7)

The nearness of the end adds an urgency to the prayers of the Reader, and a God-perspective which enables them to pray with the mind of Christ. Readers know that they are not able to fulfil the calls on them if they are not regular and disciplined in prayer. If Peter himself wrote this letter, we cannot imagine that he could forget that Jesus himself had called him to pray for assistance in the Garden of Gethsemane – and that he and his companions had fallen asleep, then later had fled or denied Jesus (see Mark 14.37ff.). If we are not to fail, it will be because God lends us his gift of discipline and we lean on him for everything.

We know, for instance, that only those who themselves spend time in the presence of God can lead others into God's presence. That means that Readers will have been disciplined in daily prayer even when the congregation may include those who find daily prayer a struggle.

Readers also realize that among the people to whom they minister are some who are 'like newborn infants' and for whom regular intercession will be an important part of the care that they exercise in relation to them. And there will be trouble ahead for all Christians – persecution figures largely in the thinking of this epistle (see for instance, 3.13ff). Christians in such circumstances also need prayer.

Do Readers aim to be people who do not allow themselves to be distracted from the discipline of prayer by things around them?

Loving people who keep no scores

> Above all maintain constant love for one another for love covers a multitude of sins. (verse 8)

Those who are not 'professionals' realize that they may never excel at the service which they offer. Since their training, though thorough, requires of them neither the same time or extent as that of other ministers in the Church, Readers are people who know that they can only minister effectively if they excel in love – which requires no formal training. Such love keeps no score of wrongs, and therefore tends to unify the Church, since it does not relish or dwell on mistakes or offences (1 Corinthians 13.5).

Readers will only minister effectively if they receive love too. One of my earliest mistakes was to turn over too many pages in *The Book of Common Prayer* and to launch into the prayer for rain in time of drought, when I should have been praying the absolution in Trinity 21 form. The love of the congregation among whom I ministered 'covered' my mistakes with their forgiveness. Their love for me gave me gentle laughter for my errors. They helped me not to take myself too seriously, and not to make the worship of God a polished performance in which they had no space for the everydayness of their worship which is often suffused with the grandeur of God.

Such love, keeping no score of wrongs, also tends to build up the Church, since it knows how to forgive until seventy times seven and thereby enables us to repent until seventy times seven, so that sin is washed away and holiness grows (Matthew 18.21-2).

'God wants a holy Church,' a bishop said to me recently, and of course he was only summing up what is to be found in the second chapter of 1 Peter: 'Rid yourselves, therefore, of all malice, and all guile, insincerity, envy, and all slander ... like living stones, let yourselves be built into a spiritual house, to be a holy priesthood ...' (1 Peter 2.1 and 5). How hard it is to confess malice, guile, insincerity, envy, slander, to an unloving Church which does not seek to cover sin by assuring us of God's forgiveness and forgiving us themselves. How easy to confess and put things right when we do so to loving people who keep no scores. Often Readers are members of churches for longer than the 'itinerant' ministry of priests; for us especially, the challenge not to remember what has been confessed and forgiven, not to keep scores, is very important.

Hospitable people who count no costs

> Be hospitable to one another without complaining. (verse 9)

Love for one another within the Christian community (or outside it) naturally leads to sharing in meals, as Jesus frequently did with many different kinds of people. In some UK cultures, such hospitality is very natural, while in others it is very rare. As a Reader, I have worshipped in churches in both kinds of culture, and the differences have been most noticeable. Even when people are used to eating in one another's homes, hospitality is most often extended more to established friends and relatives than to people who are not well known to us. And yet the chance to share the Christian life together is far greater in the informal setting of a home.

At a mission a couple of years ago I stayed in the home of a Reader and his wife who were kindness itself in making their home available to me. That Reader has since died, but his kindness lives in my memory as an example of hospitality which shared generously, did not grumble, and was undemanding of me.

Many other such stories may be told of the way in which homes are overrun by young people or by prayer groups or Alpha meals. Making space for other people in schedules which are already full of work and family is an act of hospitality in itself, and opening up the 'safe haven' of home is always costly, though always brings its own rewards – 'entertaining angels without knowing it' is how I have often experienced it (see Hebrews 13.2). There is blessing for the one who offers hospitality as well as the one who receives it.

The ancient world generally offered hospitality to travellers, and early Christian mission depended on it as itinerant ministers travelled to preach the gospel. The Church is discovering afresh in the UK how essential hospitality is to its mission, and in that context Readers have much to offer.

The outer picture

What other people see may not be immediately the inner picture which we have drawn, or the larger perspective, but the outer picture will make people ask how these things are accomplished, and the answering of that question may give us opportunity to outline the inner reality as well as the larger convictions.

Serving with the gifts of God

Serve one another with whatever gift each of you has received. (verse 10)

Readers are rarely licensed if others have not recognized in them some gift which they could use to enrich the life of the Church. When such gifts are recognized, it is possible to use them in a way which disables others who are dazzled by our abilities or giftings; or to use them in a way which shows very clearly that these gifts have been given by God to ordinary lay people, for the benefit of other ordinary lay people.

I am fortunate to worship in a parish with two other Readers. They are an inspiration to me. We have very different lives and lifestyles, and our ministries are equally varied. All of us do the 'routine' tasks, but with differing numbers of commitments which take account of our work and family circumstances. But our gifts are different, so one is more able to work with children and families, another is more used of God in the healing ministry, and my work takes me all over the place doing different things. It is a delight to work together in a team that knows one another so well, and which is so mutually supportive. It is wonderful to sit amid the congregation and receive these gifts as well as occasionally offering some myself. I do not think that we have ever felt that we were in competition with one another because we know that we are so variously gifted. And as we have grown older together we have learned from one another, and how to rely on one another.

Speaking with the very words of God

Whoever speaks must do so as one speaking the very words of God. (verse 11)

One of the most precious tasks afforded to Readers is the opportunity to preach the word of God to Christian congregations. Whether that is to two or three people in a little country church, or to several thousands who have gathered for some special occasion, every Reader has the chance to speak the very words of God. That means speaking prayerfully, humbly, expectantly – recognizing that, despite our human frailty, God can and does use us to minister his manifold grace to the people who listen to us. It is easy to think that the big occasion is more significant than the small gathering, but God showed me early in my days as a Reader that the Lord Jesus Christ is present in every congregation and that there can be no higher honour than preaching to him and to his people (Matthew 18.20).

The Church of England does not articulate very often how important it regards this task of preaching, although through publishing homilies at the time of the Reformation, and through the normal pattern of having a sermon at public worship, it testifies to the importance of this ministry. In establishing Readers who are licensed for this task, the Church of England is implying that normally congregations of lay people should not be at the mercy of people who may speak sincerely and prayerfully but about whom the Church has not in any way enquired; nor has it equipped or held them accountable in this ministry of preaching. It is true that some Readers respond to unlicensed preachers as if the Readers' rights were being violated. Nothing could be further from the truth. Readers have no rights in preaching – the pulpit belongs to the ordained person who holds responsibility in that church building or community. But Readers – inasmuch as they have been selected, trained and held accountable – show that the Church believes that some things should not normally be left to chance, and preaching is one such thing. By it, the lives of lay people may be informed or deformed, since not all will have the maturity of faith to test what they hear. By being willing to be selected, to be trained and to be account-able, the Reader is reminding the local church of the conviction of the wider Church, that preaching is a serious business. In the sermon God speaks.

Of course, that means that the Church has a responsibility to ask from time to time whether a particular Reader is still speaking the very words of God. Now that most clergy have regular reviews, perhaps the time has come for the Church to consider how that might also be offered to Readers. I do not mean by this a perfunctory form signing to say that the Reader is still active, but a serious pastoral enquiry as to the state of their Christian life. While it is undoubtedly true that God can speak through a cornflake packet, it is also true that God loves to speak through those whose lives are most clearly growing into maturity in Christ. Christian history shows that through them God's word comes most clearly into the lives of others. Anyone can tell us to live simply, loving others like Jesus did, but think of the difference between the preaching of St Francis on this area, for instance, and our own preaching.

Serving with the strength of God

Whoever serves must do so with the strength that God supplies. (verse 11)

One of the biggest questions which we face today is the question as to how we receive lay ministry (of which Readers are a part) without overburdening or exploiting the freely offered help of those who – for the most part – already have full-time work to undertake each week.

We begin with the text again, which indicates to those of us who are Readers, and who spend a great deal of our 'free time' praying, serving, preparing and taking services, and who may often find ourselves at the end of our strength, that we can find our refreshment and power to continue only in the strength which God himself supplies. No Reader who has ever helped run an 'interregnum' can fail to identify with this encouragement. Our commitment and our customary way of ministering mean that we can be tempted to take the risk of not having a day off, or of spending time which ought to be family or personal time on 'church work'.

While we need to have this conviction that God *can* strengthen us, we surely also need to ask *how* God may strengthen us – and the answer will usually be through proper sabbath, which we may take in a number of different ways. It is unlikely to be right to be involved in public ministry every week, and it is one of the precious opportunities that we have to be a regular member of a congregation as well as a person who ministers to it. This should reinforce our capacity to be effective and not diminish it.

God strengthens us for our part in the whole – and it is a part! Our overwork deprives others of their opportunity to serve in God's strength too. In this, being a Reader is like being a teacher. Everyone knows that the experienced teacher can teach, the question is whether the new pupil has the space to learn in the experienced teacher's class. God himself withdraws to leave us room, and strengthens his servants to stand aside so as to allow others to have the chance to depend on God's strength for the first time. These verses are all about mutual ministry, which requires us to receive what others offer us in God's strength as well as offering them what he has given us.

So what's the difference?

Since the passage on which this chapter has been an extended meditation was originally addressed to all Christians, we might well ask what the difference is between a Christian who is not a Reader and one who is. I hope that by now you will have realized that my answer is that the difference is simply maturity and gifting. I realize, of course, that there are Christians who are not Readers who are more mature than some Readers! What I am saying is that the Church's call to preach and lead worship should only be extended to Christians who are already mature in their faith (that is not the same as old or even being a Christian for many years!). And it should only be extended to those whom God has gifted for this particular kind of ministry.

Chapter 2

The Reader in the parish

Pat Nappin

So, at last, after the years of training and preparation you have been admitted and licensed as a Reader in what was probably a thrilling and affirming service full of encouragement and challenge. And now your ministry truly begins.

There may be questions in your mind: What will it really be like? Will my training and skills be recognized and put to use? Will the clergy accept me as a colleague? Will the congregation accept me? Can I really be a bridge between the world and the Church – between people and clergy? This chapter addresses some of the issues involved and includes snapshots of Reader ministry in a rural area and in the Diocese in Europe.

The context

Your parish will be different from mine. It may be a busy, suburban one with large congregations and a range of activities occurring during the week. It may be small with a faithful band of Christians on a housing estate, a church family in need of encouragement. It may be a village and the church the focus of community life, or a village from which most people commute, or a rural parish composed of a number of villages with several churches where congregations and ministers travel to a different church each Sunday and little contact is possible during the week.

It may be a community composed almost entirely of white 'Anglo-Saxons' or set in an area which is predominantly black or Asian. Or it might be like the parish in which I am privileged to serve, a town centre UPA parish with a Grade 1 listed parish church as well as two other churches and two aid and advice centres. It is a team ministry, where people from over twenty nationalities live and worship. Most were members of the Anglican Communion in their former countries and are familiar with the liturgy and worship of the Church of

England. They represent the world in microcosm coming from such countries as Nigeria, Hong Kong, Ghana, Sri Lanka, India, Congo, South Africa, Jamaica, Cyprus, Kosovo, Uganda, Argentina and the West Indies, among others. They include refugees and asylum seekers as well as people who were born and have lived in the area for the whole of their lives.

Being a Reader in such a parish involves bridge-building between people of different nationalities and encouraging all to value the rich diversity of cultures and spirituality that are present among them. To hear the Lord's Prayer spoken in a number of languages reminds us that God is indeed *our* Father.

Unless you have been deployed to another parish with particular needs, you will be familiar with your own church family. You know them and they know you. You may feel that that becomes a disadvantage; you may even at first, experience something of the rejection that Jesus experienced (Mark 6.1-6) when he preached to those who had known him as a boy. If this does occur then it will, in all probability, be a short-lived experience until such time as the congregation becomes used to your new role as a Reader and to seeing you robed as you lead and preach in services of worship. If you have already had the opportunity to preach on occasions during your training, or if your church is accustomed to the ministry of Readers then it may not occur at all.

Perhaps the most disconcerting experience you will encounter is that of the silence in which the sermon is received. Not that applause is expected (far from it) but often there is no apparent reaction to a sermon (whoever has preached whether bishop, vicar, Reader or visitor). This will take a while to get used to, especially if the sermons that you delivered in training received a careful and considered critique. It is helpful to ask a few trusted members of the congregation to provide you with feedback. It may be some time, if ever, before you learn that a sermon has particularly spoken to someone in need.

It is also important that the congregation should continue to know you as the lay person they have always known, sitting among them or acting as a sidesperson or choir member or whatever you were accustomed to do before being licensed. I am sure that few Readers nowadays are only present when they are 'on duty', but that temptation is firmly to be resisted.

The parish staff

Being a member of a staff team will provide support and encouragement. Your team may consist only of you and the vicar or, in a larger parish, can consist of several stipendiary clergy together with non-stipendiary ministers or ordained local ministers and one or more Readers. In some dioceses pastoral assistants and/or evangelists are also part of the authorized ministry. The team will meet on a regular basis to study, pray and worship together, to discuss pastoral needs, to plan for future services and to reflect on past as well as future events.

If you are available during the day, then membership of the weekly staff meeting will be of great benefit. If your team consists of just you and the vicar then meeting together is just as important. If you are involved in full-time employment, then regular evening or Saturday meetings will probably be arranged. If they are not, then this is an area that needs discussion with your vicar. It is important for you to 'touch base' as it were and to avoid being and feeling isolated. Collaborative ministry is increasingly the norm and is seen as the way ahead for the Church.

Occasionally an incumbent has not thought through the difference that having a Reader colleague is likely to make to his/her own ministry and may find the reality of sharing their ministry a difficulty. You will need to be sensitive in the way that you approach the situation. Most dioceses have local advisers in place to support Readers in their ministry, and they can help to resolve problems where these occur.

Areas of work

All incumbents will have drawn up a Working Agreement with the new Reader before admission and licensing. This will outline the areas of ministry in which the Reader will be involved and the frequency of that involvement. You may feel that you can commit yourself to preaching on an agreed basis, perhaps once a month initially. Plans can be made as to the services in which you will be involved and the precise nature of your involvement in them. It might be leading the service or preaching, leading the prayers, reading the lessons, administering the sacrament or helping other members of the church to do so.

You may be able (subject, as Canon E 4 indicates, to the permission of the incumbent and the goodwill of the families – see the Appendix, page 63) to officiate at funerals and visit the bereaved family. This may be a time when people feel that they can relate to a lay person more easily than to one of the clergy. It may also be an occasion, where the Reader has known the family for some years and can be an important link between them and the clergy. At a time of distress it can be reassuring to have someone you know as the minister. You may feel that this will be a daunting experience but in actual fact it can be one of the most fulfilling aspects of your ministry as a Reader. It is a time when you and the bereaved person or family draw closer together, and it is generally greatly appreciated.

The agreement will also indicate the teaching responsibilities that you will undertake, that is, with Bible study or house groups or preparation for baptism, marriage or confirmation. The pastoral aspects of your ministry will also be planned – visiting of the sick, the housebound and other members of the congregation, to be involved with the young people or special groups for men or women. Much will depend on your own circumstances and availability.

In the countryside

Life for the Reader living in a rural community may be very different, with little contact with some church communities other than at services and one writes:

> A Reader's check-list is a good idea, whether or not it is actually written down. What times? Which church buildings? What types of service? Can I use the same sermon each time? Do they have hymns? Which hymn book? Will there be someone to play? Are there pew Bibles? Which version of the Bible? Has it changed since last time? (At one of 'my' churches they seem to alternate Bible versions.) It is the same for Readers everywhere. In advance, get as much information as you can and on the day, be prepared for anything. (Like the time I was doing the sermon only and as we approached the church door, the vicar told me there was a baptism – no sermon has been more radically revised during delivery!)

> Wherever I take a service, it involves a car journey. I live on the edge of my deanery and the nearest church building is eight miles away – the furthest can involve an hour's driving. Public transport is a rarity, even on weekdays.

> If, as a Reader, I am taking Morning Prayer or family services I might also want to consider where there will be a eucharistic service for me to attend. This involves more pre-planning; because for many country parish churches service times vary from week to week as vicars seek to serve multi-parish benefices. So in addition to a large armful of prayer/collect/hymn books, I usually take a flask of coffee and I expect to spend part of Sunday morning sitting in a lay-by or a car park. Even if I am taking only one service, it is wise to allow extra travelling time in case a shepherd has decided that a quiet Sunday morning is just the time for moving a flock of sheep between fields.

> Although, after a gap of several weeks, I may have difficulty remembering whether a particular congregation sing the Venite and say the Benedicite, or vice versa; there is clear continuity in other matters –

the progress of hospital treatment, the prices for stock taken to auction, the effects of the weather on tourists and agricultural crops ... Their concern for me echoes my concern for them and the talk over home-made scones after the service may be practical, theological or pastoral. Isolated farming families may see no one during the week and Sunday services are important for the community and socially. They are a time for worship, but they are also a time for giving back borrowed equipment, exchanging library books and for handing over home-grown rhubarb – often the Reader also comes away with fresh vegetables, free range eggs and newly cut flowers. Love in action – what need is there for sermons?!

In Europe

Your experience may be quite different from that Reader's, but is unlikely to compare in any way with this Reader in the Diocese in Europe who, unable to find an Anglican church in which to worship, has been the key person in the building up of a congregation, while at the same time training as a Reader:

> I have lived and taught in Spain for over twenty-five years but I have never lived within worshipping distance of an Anglican church. There is no Anglican church on this island so after much prayer and con-sultation the congregation of La Palma was formed and I was licensed as Reader in the year 2000.
>
> La Palma, is one of the seven Canary Islands and is in the province of Tenerife which is a thirty-minute plane trip away or a five-hour one by ferry. We hold a service of Morning Prayer every Sunday at the Roman Catholic church of St Martin de Porres. The church is only used by the Catholic community once a year on St Martin's Day, so we virtually have a free hand in its use. Every third Saturday we have a Holy Communion service, which is led by the chaplain of All Saints, Tenerife, and the church to which we belong. Our congregation covers the priest's travel expenses. There is no resident chaplain at present so we have had a series of locums until a permanent one is appointed.
>
> La Palma has a population of about 80,000 and ten per cent of this number are German. The British population is minute, but our English service attracts not only the British but also some Germans, Dutch and Americans. Some of our elderly worshippers go back to their country of origin in the summer months and we also have visitors who are here on holiday. I suppose you could call us a 'floating' congregation since we never quite know how many of us there will be, who is

permanent or who is just passing through. Perhaps that is part of the joy I feel to be able to serve God by leading the services in this somewhat unusual setting.

We are blessed to be able to worship in such idyllic surroundings although the church has no electricity or toilet facilities; our portable organ works on batteries. St Paul tells us that we are all part of the body of Christ – working together in unity of spirit – and indeed there are so many different skills and gifts in our small congregation. I am very much part of a team here although we have sometimes felt geographically isolated, particularly when the airport is closed because of bad climatic conditions. We have in the past not been able to have a Holy Communion service for months.

It is at times like these that I feel it essential to be able to update my skills by attending courses in the UK. The Selwyn one I attended in Cambridge this year was invaluable, not only as regards the content and quality of the course material but the fact that I was able to meet so many other Readers and share our experiences.

So far, our congregation has had a wedding blessing celebrated when the priest came over from Tenerife and a baptism and confirmation ceremony were celebrated in Tenerife and members of our congregation went over there. We should like to think that eventually we would be large enough to require the services of a resident chaplain. Time will tell.

I think I can truly say that the formation of our congregation has been the answer to much prayer. With Jesus here in our midst where else can we go if not firmly forward?

A bridge ministry

Both those Readers act as 'bridges' into their local community, scattered as they are. A bridge is what all Readers are – a bridge between lay and ordained, a bridge between the Church and the world, a bridge between the world of work and the home, a bridge between individual members of the church family. Above all, Readers are a help and a bridge for those who seek to find God and who are more ready to discuss their tentative steps towards faith with a lay person rather than one of the clergy. So being a Reader is challenging and leads one into situations and areas that are unexpected. It is there that your own walk with God is of crucial importance.

It is important for your own spiritual well-being that you have the time and space for your own worship and Bible study, and there may be times when you have to say 'no' to a request for assistance.

It is all too easy to find yourself overworked, though some Readers complain of being underemployed. Whenever either of these situations arises, it is important to discuss it with your incumbent and seek a solution. Inevitably, there will be occasions, perhaps through illness, when you are called upon to assist or preach at short notice. This is unlikely to occur until you have had some experience, but most Readers know of the need for flexibility.

In addition to your regular worship in your own parish, it is good to get right away and spend time on retreat. A time when the pressures of family and work and the parish can be put to one side and the time can be spent with God. I value greatly my own experience of a week spent in the Sinai desert where there was nothing and no one (apart from our small group) to come between us and God. For those whose responsibilities are such that they find it difficult to be away, then there are always opportunities for weekend or day retreats. These are times for rest, reflection and recreation.

It is also important, if you are employed, that work does not suffer because of your ministry as a Reader. To find yourself tired because you have not used a day off for that purpose, or failing to complete necessary preparation (e.g., for school lessons, etc.) because you were preparing a sermon, will be inappropriate. Keeping too many balls in the air at once may be possible some of the time but not always, and sermons, in particular, can take a great deal of time to prepare well.

Continuing training

But however your ministry develops and whatever direction it takes, your need for ongoing training – CME (Continuing Ministerial Training), as it is called, will continue. Some dioceses provide helpful, worthwhile training. Some of it may be held jointly with the clergy and this may be the most helpful of all, when you can discuss common concerns in your ministries. Some dioceses offer annual grants, which vary in amount. The Central Readers' Council administers several funds and may be able to assist with the costs of courses, which are supported by the warden of Readers in the diocese. Application forms can be obtained from the office in Church House, Westminster, London. The course will need to be one that will enrich and enable the Reader's ministry.

The Council publishes a quarterly magazine containing articles, book reviews and resources of use to Readers. This is generally paid for by the diocese but can also be purchased by individual Readers in those dioceses that do not do so. Copies can also be sent to Readers who live in the Diocese of Europe or other parts of the Anglican Communion. There is also a web site which provides information for enquirers as well as serving Readers (*www.readers.cofe.anglican.org*).

To sum up

Being a Reader is a challenging, exciting and fulfilling ministry and nowhere more so than in the parish. It is a partnership in every sense of the word. In my experience it is one that brings great joy to the Reader and can act as a stimulus for other lay people to realize the possibilities of lay ministry that exist in the Church. The Reader can be a model of such ministry and opens the way for others to respond to the challenges and opportunities of greater participation and partnership in the mission of the Church.

Chapter 3

Readers at work

Andrew Britton

A Reader is licensed to a particular parish, and is given individual responsibilities within that parish, such as preaching, leading worship or organizing study groups. But the call to Reader ministry will make a difference to the whole of life – to relationships with family and friends, to leisure time and to work. Indeed some Readers would say that ministry in the world outside is more important to them than ministry to their local congregation. Ideally the two sides of ministry support one another, and fit naturally together.

Reader ministry can go well with virtually any kind of (honest!) work. This chapter is not just about the paid work that is done by those in regular employment. Equally significant is the relation of Reader ministry to the unpaid work of bringing up a family, caring for the young and the old, the work of a student, or voluntary work undertaken in one's spare time or in retirement. In every case, the personal commitment and the theological training which come with Reader ministry can motivate and guide us in the service which we offer to God and to our neighbours in our lives as a whole.

This chapter begins with some reflections on the ethics or theology of work. From this follows a section on the consequences for our working lives, which come as a result of being a Reader. This includes a comparison between the way that Readers are likely to be regarded by those alongside whom they work with the perception of priests in secular employment. Many Readers do work for the Church which might seem to be essentially secular in character: they are churchwardens, PCC secretaries, members of church committees and so on. A special section of the chapter is devoted to them. Then we look at the influence in the opposite direction. How does a secular occupation affect the sermons we preach or the themes we introduce into public worship? The chapter concludes with a discussion of possible conflicts between the demands of ministry and the demands of work. How can the unity of life and service be maintained in a compartmentalized world?

The ethics and theology of work

The same word, 'vocation', is commonly used for a call to the service of God and for a particular occupation or trade. This reflects the Christian understanding that all good work is pleasing to God, that work can be seen as a form of prayer, and that we fulfil ourselves best by serving others. From this there follows both a right and a duty to work, whether that is in paid employment or not.

The theological grounds for a Christian work ethic can be found in both creation and redemption. God works, and our efforts can be seen as cooperation with him, in the making and preserving of the world. Such labour is not in vain if God can use it for his purposes. In the book of Genesis, Adam is given the work of a gardener (Genesis 2.15). This job is assigned to him before the Fall, so work is to be seen as an expression of human nature and a reflection of the image of God in us (Genesis 1.27), not as a punishment for sin. The penalty which is imposed after the Fall is that work becomes a burden as well as a blessing (Genesis 3.17-19).

We share, in a sense, in the saving work of Christ when we become the servants of others in love and in humility. Even the work of a slave, washing the feet of his master, can be seen in this light. We work to ease the burdens of others, sharing their suffering and offering ourselves in their service. This aspect of work may be most easy to discern in occupations like nursing or counselling where help is offered directly, but the model is of much more general application. The work may consist of making or selling a product that contributes to the comfort and well-being of others. If it can be said to make the world a better place, then it can be described as, in some small part, redemptive.

Increasingly the tasks performed by human hands and brains are being taken over by machines. This has led some to talk of 'the end of work'. It would be better to say that work is gradually changing its character, and in some respects at least, the change is for the better. If machines can take over some of the drudgery, mental as well as physical, the creative and redemptive aspects of work may become more evident. Machines cannot be creative in the same sense as human minds or spirits; machines cannot enter into relationships or express redemptive love. One way or another, work goes on so long as there is human need to be met, and human capability to meet it.[1]

The fact that much work is done for a wage does not change any of this. We live in a market economy and have little chance of opting out of it. One reason to work is, of course, to earn a living. The organizations that we work for have also to pay their way. Yet, as Christians, we must be aware of the ultimate purpose of good work, which is to produce good things, and not just to make money.

It seems right to assume that many, perhaps most, of those who are called to Reader ministry will be called to some other work as well. They will have not one 'vocation', but two or more. There are few full-time Readers, although some of those who have retired from secular employment may find themselves in that position at times. Most have to find the right balance between their several callings. If no such balance can be found, the result may well be overwork.

It is part of the theology of work that God himself rested on the last day of the week. The observation of the Sabbath was extremely important to the writers of the Old Testament. In the New Testament, the story of Mary and Martha clearly teaches us that work is not the only, or the most essential, part of Christian life (Luke 10.38-42). Jesus himself admired the birds because they do not sow or reap or store away in barns, and the lilies of the field that do not labour or spin (Matthew 6.25-34). We live in a society that seems to admire overwork, that values high earnings and driving ambition. None of these sits easily with Christian teaching, or with the pattern of Reader ministry.

Readers in the workplace

Theology is the same for Readers as it is for any other Christian. Everything that can be said about Christian attitudes to work applies to Readers, no more and no less, than it does to all church members. Perhaps the point to emphasize is that Readers should never forget that their work in a secular context is service of God no less than their service in church. There is a temptation to regard it as no more than a distraction, no more than a means of financial support, while our hearts and minds are centred on the parish. That would be to retreat from one of the great challenges and opportunities of ministry and discipleship.

Readers do not wear dog collars, or style themselves as 'reverend'. A few wear some small badge of office, but most of us have no distinguishing mark at all. Our ministry as Readers is likely, therefore, to be unknown to most of our fellow workers and business associates. Its significance will be understood and acknowledged by few. In this, our position is rather different from that of a 'worker priest', a non-stipendiary or minister in secular employment.

Paradoxically, Reader ministry is special, precisely because it is ordinary. We are not priests and cannot, in the same way, pronounce the blessing or forgiveness of God; but we can stand beside other lay men and women asking for blessing and forgiveness on us all. That is how the difference appears in the context of a church service. There is a similar difference in the weekday world. We are not 'vicars', as some of our colleagues would put it. The

21

distinction between Christian ministries may be dimly perceived even by those who have no Christian faith or allegiance at all. This can be an opportunity rather than a limitation. We may be seen as people who take their religion seriously, while still remaining sufficiently 'worldly' in outlook to be approachable.

Having said this, the opportunities for work-place evangelism should not be exaggerated. It is always tricky, and sometimes counter-productive, to preach uninvited to one's boss or to one's staff. Relationships at work are governed by certain conventions and tacit understandings which limit the degree of human contact which is actually made. Sometimes it is possible, and right, to convert such relationships into real personal encounters, but this can never be taken for granted. One can never speak of one's faith effectively when pretending to a relationship that does not really exist. For this purpose many of those we deal with at work are no more than strangers to us – and it would be wrong to address them in any other way. It is true that we have a licence to preach the gospel, but that does not give us a position within the work community that all others can be expected to recognize or respect.

We can, and should, convey the gospel by example as well as by word. In some degree the opinion of Christianity that is formed by the public depends on the way that known Christians behave in the face of ordinary situations and problems, successes and failures, such as everyone meets from day to day. As Readers we are more likely to be known as Christians than we otherwise would be. Our lives should be, as best we can manage, exemplary.

All occupations involve ethical dilemmas. It cannot be said that, in business, honesty is always and without exception the best policy. It is a hard competitive world, where survival may depend on being ruthless. It is not always possible to be kind to one's staff and to keep labour costs under control. The best product may not be the most profitable product to make or to sell, and so on. It is not easy to be wise (or shrewd) as a serpent and harmless (or innocent) as a dove – and not the other way round (see Matthew 10.16)!

Working for the Church

St Paul, writing to the Romans, referred to the variety of gifts that are needed in the Church. He mentioned preaching, teaching and pastoral care, as would be expected. But he also mentioned administration (Romans 12.3-8 and see also 1 Corinthians 12.27-31 especially verse 28). This is a great comfort to those who serve on bodies like the PCC or the Diocesan Board of Finance. We are, no doubt, what St Paul meant by the parts of the body that are 'less seemly (or honourable) than the rest' – we are the kidneys or the lesser intestines. But he said, rightly, that we are indispensable to the body as a whole (1 Corinthians 12.21-6).

One might suppose that administration of this kind is 'churchy' enough to belong to the world of Sunday worship rather than the weekday world of work. It may indeed be true that church business meetings start and finish with a short prayer. But what comes between those prayers may be little different from any other business committee. Churches have to know what is 'the bottom line' just as companies do; their accounts have to add up. They may be employers in dispute with their employees. As charities they compete for funds with other good causes. They have legal obligations as well as moral and spiritual ones.

Churches need many of the same skills and types of experience as are required in secular employment. They have buildings to maintain, so they need architects, plumbers and cleaners. They handle money, so they need accountants, clerks and sometimes security guards. Worship itself may involve organists, florists or bell-ringers. This is all work, although most of it is unpaid. Some of it is done by Readers.

One might ask what, if anything, one gains from being a Reader if one's job is to chair a church committee, or to sell cakes at the Christmas fair. Certainly it could not be a requirement for such jobs that one undertakes three years of theological training. Yet that training surely is helpful and relevant. Much of what has been said about the role of a Reader in a secular occupation can be said, with even more force, about similar jobs which are done for a church organization. The difference is that this is an explicitly Christian organization, and therefore itself committed to a Christian ethic of work. The dilemmas are all still there, but they face the organization as a whole rather than just the individual worker or employee. The organization itself should be exemplary, demonstrating to the world how the Christian life can be lived in the world, and what difference it makes in practice. The Reader should be relatively well equipped to handle the very real difficulties which that can involve.

Preaching about work

Most congregations want to hear sermons that are relevant to their weekday lives; not many preachers provide them. Readers are often better able than the clergy to fill this gap. They have not just studied the theology of work, and the Christian work ethic, they have tried to put them into practice, and they know from their own experience how difficult it can be.

The Gospels are full of stories taken from the working lives of the community in which the early Church was set. They are about farmers, shepherds, fishermen,

23

housewives, day labourers, traders and money-lenders. At least one of the sayings of Jesus seems to be derived from his own occupation as a carpenter (Matthew 7.3-5). There must be plenty of material for new parables in, for example, computer programming, mobile telephones and personal finance.

Perhaps one should preach on every occasion about the application of the gospel to the contemporary world. Perhaps there should be illustrations from the world of work in every sermon. But there are also some special days when teaching on such issues is most obviously appropriate. One such occasion is Rogation Sunday. This is the day when we ask God's blessing on the sowing of the seed. It is therefore, to start with, an agricultural festival, and that will still be the main focus, especially in a rural parish. But it has come to be a festival of work and production, more broadly defined. People are encouraged to think and to pray about their own part in production, as well as the efforts of others on which they depend. In every production process there is likely to be something analogous to the sowing of seed; and every kind of production is dependent on God's blessing for its abundance.

Later in the year comes Harvest Festival, another agricultural occasion often adapted to celebrate fruitfulness of every kind. Along with the sheaves of corn, one can decorate the church with the produce of industry and commerce. This need not mean an unquestioning endorsement of everything that might be called 'wealth creation' today. Indeed the suggestion that some token of one's output should be on show in church, as an offering to God, may provoke some awareness of its uncertain value. But, whatever the real value of the product, this is an acknowledgement that nothing at all could be produced without God's providence.

A very different kind of service might be held on Unemployment Sunday, which is the Sunday before Lent.[2] The meaning of work is seldom as evident as it becomes to those who look for it in vain. People who are unemployed do not only lack income; they are prevented from making their contribution to society, they feel devalued as well as frustrated. They frequently become severely depressed, sometimes suicidal. The importance attached to work in Christian ethics and theology implies that no one should be deprived of the opportunity to share in it. At the same time we need to stress that those who are out of work are not in fact devalued in the eyes of God. We do not have to work to earn our salvation. Rather we seek to work as a way of expressing our thanks for the salvation which comes to us as a free gift. A Reader who has personal experience of involuntary unemployment will often be the best person to preach on such a theme.

The danger with these special occasions is that work is treated as a topic for prayer and thanksgiving at those times alone. The world of work should be taken right to the heart of worship every Sunday. It should be taken for granted that we pray at all the main services for guidance in our own work, for the true prosperity of our community, for the poor, the overburdened and for those who feel themselves to be rejected. The Eucharist is always an occasion to offer to God 'the work of human hands', symbolized as bread and wine. We then receive those gifts back from God transformed into the body and blood of Christ. At the end of the service we are told to go in peace to love and serve the Lord.

The Church and the world

The really big questions raised in this chapter have been about the relationship of the Church, the Christian community, to the society in which we live. These are questions which can vex all Christians, since all of us live in the world (including the clergy!) as well as in the Church. How can our lives be unified? How can we escape from the bad faith involved in trying to serve two masters?

There seem to be several different models of Church and society present in the Bible. In much of the Old Testament it is assumed that the whole nation of Israel serves God and is in a covenant relationship with him. The prophets may berate the people for their disobedience, but they are calling for the renewal of a relationship which is established and understood. In much of the New Testament, on the other hand, the world, meaning society at large, is seen as in the power of evil. God's children are called individually to separate themselves from this society and become citizens of God's kingdom instead.

But which of these models can we apply to our own country today? The Old Testament model does not seem to fit well, now that we find ourselves in a pluralist society. But the New Testament picture of the early Church does not fit exactly either. We live in a post-Christian society, rather than a pagan one. The requirement still is to live in the world but not to belong to it (John 17.14-19). Each generation has to work out for itself quite what that will mean in practice.

Readers face this requirement more clearly than most church members, as we seek to follow our two (or more) vocations at once. We live on the borderline, or the interface, where two sets of ideals and assumptions face each other. We must not just sit on the fence; we must not fall between two stools; we cannot stand with one foot in each camp – there is no shortage of appropriate metaphors!

Life on a borderline can be stimulating as well as confusing. The two sides of our ministry can support one another as well as conflict. The key to success is to recognize that God is with us on *both* sides of the divide, 'out there' in the world as well as 'here' in the relative safety of the Church. It may not always be easy to discern his presence, or to understand what he is doing, but he has his purposes which we must support as best we can. But, let us not forget that it may not be much easier to see what he is doing in the Church itself.

For some of us at least, this borderland is the best place to live. We need the life and worship of the Church to prevent us from despairing at (or conniving with) the sinfulness of the world which assails us every day; we need the world and our calling to work in it to prevent us from suffocating in the close atmosphere of a church when it turns in on itself. That may be why Reader ministry seems the right one for so many people today.

Chapter 4

The Reader as preacher

Margaret Hounsham

> The Lord God has spoken: who can but prophesy? (Amos 3.8b)

By our baptism we are welcomed into the Church as members. But the Church is not a club, and we are not just club members. We cannot expect simply to make free use of the facilities made available to us by the privilege of membership. As baptized Christians we become part of 'the priesthood of all believers' (see 1 Peter 2.9). Being a baptized Christian demands an active response. Our response is to go out and make Christ known to others. Bringing good news is a task that is entrusted to every Christian.

For most Christians this task is an informal one. The way they live and the conversations they have with others are their opportunity for making Christ known. For others the task is based on more formal foundations. In the Church of England it is expected that those who preach sermons in church will hold a licence from their bishop to do so (although an occasional homily from unlicensed people is acceptable). The Reader's Licence is an authorization from the bishop to preach regularly as lay people. Indeed, Reader ministry is the flagship lay order and it is distinguished as being fully recognized by Canon Law (see Appendix, page 63).

Preaching is the primary task of the Reader.[1] This is clear from selection where ability to preach is a one of the important criteria. Preaching is also given particular mention in the Bishops' Regulations for Reader Ministry.

Why do we need Readers to preach?

Readers (with Accredited Lay Workers and Church Army Officers) are the only lay people who may preach regularly in the Church of England and they preach from a life that is both within and outside the body of the Church. They are at one time both local and part of the wider Church and they can also bring to the local church an awareness of worldly affairs from daily life in many different spheres.

Readers and the Bible

The Reader is reading the Bible on behalf of the congregation and is then in a position to 'break open' the word of the Bible that may be difficult to grasp. In this role Readers can point the Church to the truth that the Bible is for all, not just for experts.

Readers and the clergy

Readers should also be able to ask difficult questions that keep clergy alert and prepared to offer their best. The clergy need preachers to listen to as much as any other Christian. Readers are well placed to be asking those questions and preaching to the clergy for the benefit of the whole Church.[2]

Readers and other lay people

If the preaching of Readers as lay people is seen as a general practice in the Church of England then other lay people may consider taking their place in 'the priesthood of all believers', in the work of all lay people, not just those with an accredited ministry.

Readers in a parish staff team

There is a responsibility for Readers to keep in fine balance that place they hold between staff and congregation. The process of licensing the Reader must not be seen as a moment when that person leaves the pew never to return. If the Reader leaves the robes in the vestry and spends the occasional Sunday in the pew in everyday dress the benefits will be enormous. A productive two-way communication between the team and the congregation will help all the preachers in a parish team to maintain an awareness of the needs and anxieties of the congregation. The special context in which Readers operate has to be seen as a distinctive opportunity. Too often, however, Readers are seen as 'pretend' vicars, and some have been guilty of setting themselves up in that way. Alternatively, Readers have, in the past, been seen as useful gap-fillers or as the vicar's helper, who will stand aside when the vicar is available. Such attitudes lead to the assumption that Reader ministry is not a proper or complete ministry of the Church. It has sometimes even been used as a training period for candidates for ordination, or even a consolation for those who are not selected as ordinands. Assuming that these valuable lay ministers are another form of clergy reduces the scope of the preaching of the Church, and leads to the risk that Readers may try to conform to what they see as a conventional way of preaching. Thus, congregations are deprived of the possible riches of a variety of preaching voices.

Training Readers as lay preachers

One way to avoid losing sight of the lay status of Readers, and to prevent the risk of confusing Readers with clergy, is for Readers to be given training that addresses their unique calling and equips them to undertake a preaching ministry with a very special foundation. The question of Reader training is addressed in another chapter of this book. The implications of training for Readers as preachers do, however, have to be given specific consideration.

Scripture

The Bible is a difficult book to read without any guidance. To preach straight from Scripture without a guide to its complex contexts and the way in which history has left its mark, would be to invite inaccuracy or even heresy to be preached. It is also much easier for people to approach a preaching ministry if they are confident of their grasp of knowledge of the books of the Bible, the history of how they came to be written and the way each book relates to the other books in the Bible.

Church history and doctrine

Preachers do not stand alone but are part of the company of preachers through history. The Church has spent two thousand years growing and forming. Anyone who preaches in the Church today benefits from understanding their place in the whole history of the Church, and study of history helps them to understand the tradition of their own local church.

Christian ethics

Training Readers as preachers should include some exploration of moral issues and the Christian response to moral dilemmas, both within the local community and exploring the implications for Christians of world events. Congregations want to know what it is they must do to respond to the love of God. Occasionally preachers may have to challenge unChristian behaviour.

Self-awareness

Academic modules are only one aspect of the training of a preacher. I have outlined above the reason why it is important for Readers to preach. The special viewpoint that Readers offer is of benefit to the whole preaching of the Church. In addition to this, every person has a unique viewpoint because we are all different. Preachers must celebrate their unique voice and learn to use it to best effect.[3] Trainees can benefit from group work or from self-examination. A helpful way to do this is on residential retreats.

Prayer and spirituality

The residential retreat is vital for another reason. The word of a preacher will never become the Word of God without prayer. It is essential for a preacher to spend time simply being with God in order to listen. It is helpful to have the support of someone (spiritual director or soul-friend) to meet with regularly in order to offer one's best as a preacher.

Liturgy

The sermon does not stand alone and isolated. There is no such thing as a 'sermon slot' because the sermon is an integral part of the whole service. A preacher needs to have an understanding of the rhythm and flow of Christian worship. Every service is built around a central theme which may be related to the Scripture reading or the collect for that day. The sermon must fit in seamlessly. Different services will suggest different types of sermon. The sermon for a large family Eucharist will not be the same as the sermon for a quiet evensong for six or seven people.

Preaching

Those who are exploring a vocation as a Reader may have many questions:

How does it feel to stand in front of a congregation?

Many training programmes now include preaching practice, preferably in a real church setting but in small groups of fellow trainees. In such a setting it is helpful to be able to try out the different places to preach from. Some people prefer to use a pulpit but others find that a daunting place to be, looking down at the congregation from above (with a fine view of all the expectant faces, but also a clear view of the person at the back examining the ceiling).[4] It is common to find preachers standing at a lectern in the front of the centre aisle of a church, preaching in among the people.

Standing up to preach leads to a variety of feelings. There is certainly a rush of adrenalin. To be called to preach is a privilege and a challenge and the people before the preacher deserve to hear the good news. The effect of the adrenalin is mixed. It boosts the ego ('I'm the one they've come to hear!'), and leads to a crisis of confidence ('I'll never be good enough.'). It is helpful to build a new preacher's confidence gently, starting with short homilies at informal services and working up to a regular preaching ministry at mainstream services such as the family Eucharist. Many training programmes rely on the support of the parish incumbent to offer this building level of experience.

Where on earth do I start?

Prayer, of course! Then, in general, a sermon will start from one of the Scripture texts to be read at the service. Preparation for a sermon means reading Scripture in a special way. The Bible is not being read as part of a prayer time or as preparation for a Bible study group and certainly not as if to write an essay! It is helpful to start with a first 'go', reading the text, possibly out loud. Then ask some key questions: What is striking about the passage? What is amazing? What questions are raised? What is attractive? It is important to resist the temptation to turn to a commentary or Bible handbook at this stage.

After the first reading, it is important to leave the desk and go away for some time to mull over the questions and the text. Often events in the course of daily life will trigger connections with the reading. It is advisable not to return to the text for a few days, but then return and study a little deeper, still without a commentary. Find out about what is written in the Bible before and after the verses specified for the reading. Research the historical background behind the text.

Now it is possible to go to a commentary and to see what someone else's view of the text adds to your own personal impressions. At this stage the passage may have offered an insight or it may not yet have yielded fruit. Be prepared to go away and wait. Nearly every passage will eventually 'pop' – give up a surprise or an insight that can be worked on to produce a sermon.[5]

What is involved in writing a sermon?

The second stage of preparation is writing a script for the sermon. Do not be tempted to rely on preaching off the cuff. Most experienced preachers who seem to preach without notes will have started from a carefully prepared script that was then consigned to memory. Consider the type of sermon the passage seems to lend itself to. Will this be a carefully structured argument, an idea developed through a narrative or story or will it be an idea put across using an image?[6] Start by writing down every idea that arises from the preparation of the text. Now refine those ideas and cut out most of them!

31

Many sermons try to include every point that comes from a text. Resist the temptation – in a preaching ministry there will be plenty of chances to preach on the passage again and to use those ideas then. Form your thoughts into a series of headings that link with each other. It should be possible to outline the basic message that has been distilled down from this work into a sentence of no more than twenty words. This is 'the big idea'. What is 'the big idea' going to do? In other words, what is the aim of the sermon – the effect that you want it to have on the listeners?

Bearing in mind your aim, write a first draft using the headings as the guideline. Open by grasping the attention of the congregation. It is possible to lose the listeners within the first few seconds of a sermon by not opening creatively enough. Ensure that the main body of the text progresses smoothly through its ideas. If there are illustrations, do not use too many and introduce them so that they do not interrupt the flow of thought. Every sermon must in some way, explicitly or implicitly, include the good news that Christ died and rose again. For a sermon at a Eucharist the preacher is preparing the congregation to be ready to receive the sacrament by being aware of the presence of Christ.

It is not necessary to offer concrete truths or answers to all the questions the congregation may be asking. The best sermons are those where the preacher leaves the listeners to work things out for themselves. Jesus never handed out teaching on a plate. His parables always left the audience guessing. He even finished some with a question – 'Who do you think this man's neighbour was?' At the preparation stage it is essential to be ruthless. If you are working at a computer or word processor do not be afraid of the delete button.

Now take the first draft and read it out loud – this is where the rest of the household will know that you have gone mad! Now go away and leave the sermon.

Return to the sermon and read it again. It is highly likely that it will now be necessary to rewrite it radically. If it is totally unsatisfactory, start again. When it is finished, read it and reread it several times so that it is very familiar.

How do I prepare for delivering the sermon?

Spend some time in the church while it is empty. Stand at the place where you will preach and become accustomed to the way it feels. If using a pulpit check what it feels like to climb the stairs in robes. While the church is empty it is also helpful to imagine the people who will be sitting in the congregation at the service. Go and sit in various places around the church and decide what it might feel like to be the person who usually sits there. What is that person's view of the place where the preacher stands? How might the preacher's words be affected by the things that are going on in that person's life?[7]

Is there a microphone and how is it switched on? Practise using a microphone. This is a special skill. Do not put your mouth too close to the microphone as this distorts the words, but make sure that you are close enough for your voice to register. Some sound systems make the words in a sentence melt together, so practise speaking slightly more slowly and leaving space between each individual word. If the church uses a clip-on radio microphone then ensure it is switched on and do not clip it to a crisp fold of your robes as this will register over the system as an annoying rustling sound. Remember, if a sound system is fitted in a church it is usually so that the hard of hearing can listen on a loop system. This cuts out all the noise except the voice of the person speaking. *Do not be tempted to think that a microphone is not necessary.*

Just before the start of the service the preacher is in need of prayer again. Find a place where you can keep silence and offer the sermon to God (at this stage it often seems depressingly inadequate and it is too late now to rewrite it!).

When standing before the congregation, either in the pulpit or in front of the nave, stand with shoulders back and feet slightly apart and breathe deeply before you start. Preachers usually begin with an opening prayer ('May the words of my mouth and the thoughts of our hearts be acceptable in your sight, O Lord') This is not just a routine formula. For the preacher this is a prayer from the heart.

The reason for reading the script over and over is so that the sermon can be delivered without being tied down to reading the words too closely. It is essential to speak looking up at the people you are addressing and to make eye contact with as many as possible around the church. (In Parliament it is a source of derision if an MP is caught reading too closely from a prepared script and leads to shouts of 'Reading! Reading!' It is often a temptation to shout this out at a preacher.) Try not to indulge in any nervous habits such as pushing back spectacles on the nose, or swaying as you speak. These habits can be distracting to those who are watching.

Where can I get help?

Trainee Readers can find help from the training department of their diocese. Those involved in Reader training are anxious to produce competent preachers with the best possible skills. The parish incumbent will also usually be of help. In the early stages the incumbent would be the person to ask for advice when in the process of preparing a sermon. They would usually also be happy to offer advice after the sermon about improvements that could be made for the next sermon. It is good to set up a system of gaining feedback after preaching. Any preacher would be wise to ask various members of the congregation to comment (members of one's family are often the most honest!), but helpful feedback comes from others in the parish who also preach. Feedback needs to include the content of the sermon, the structure of the sermon and even the way you stand and any nervous habits you may have developed.

Preaching in today's changing world

We live in a culture where change is fast and frequent. The craft of preaching has been affected as much as any other form of communication by this speed of change which has accelerated over the last fifty years or so. To keep abreast of the times we must continuously review the way we preach.

The way things were

The preachers of the nineteenth century and earlier were preaching to people who, in general, knew their place in the social hierarchy and tended to stick where they were. They knew the rules and usually obeyed them. The sermons that were preached in the nineteenth century reflect this attitude. Preachers studied the Bible to find answers and then preached the answers in their sermons. In general the listeners were happy to accept the word of the preacher as that of an expert.

What has changed?

Nowadays the structures of society are not so clearly defined. The consumer society makes demands more than it obeys rules. People assert their rights, and there is a general maxim that everyone has their own personal understanding of truth which may not be the same as their neighbour's truth. Truth has been reduced to another commodity in a consumer age.

We need to be conscious that there has been dramatic change in the way we look at information, whether it is a newspaper article, a novel or the text of Scripture. Communication in the twentieth century went through an astonishing evolution, so that where once there was only the printed word, we now have radio and television, films, telecommunications including mobile phones, the Internet and emails and a proliferation of advertising in all media, all of which has influenced language and the way people respond to information.

The present-day media bombard our congregations with images of every kind, often very quickly moving from one image to the next. Radio presenters have developed skills in creating word pictures, and images that listeners build in their imaginations. Even when information is still in the form of words, the information is packaged in short, pithy 'bites' of sound. Attention span has been reduced to a correspondingly short time. A preacher can no longer rely on holding a congregation's attention for twenty minutes (let alone forty minutes), although some churches do expect sermons of this length. The media no longer use the 'essay' style to make a point. Instead there is widespread use of story to put across an idea.

In short, we can no longer preach as if nothing has changed, because our congregations have developed different listening habits. Readers who are engaged with various aspects of twenty-first century communication in their working lives are a vital resource for the rest of the Church in responding to change.

One aspect of this change that helps to show its extent is in the transition from *thinking* to *feeling*. In the past there was a danger that faith was linked only to knowledge. Knowledge meant a sound understanding of Scripture and even some learning about the history of the Bible and of the history of the times of Jesus. Faith was an agreement of the mind. Nowadays it is understood that faith is more than that. It involves experience and feelings. Faith is a response of the heart. This is good news for ordinary Christians who may have struggled in the past with the intellectual demands made on them by preachers. The implications for preachers about living in a time of change have been explored by writers who have researched preaching as a discipline (this is known as homiletics) over the last few decades and come up with new approaches to the task of preaching. Such new approaches have been described as 'the new homiletic'.[8]

The new homiletic

Many people recognize the start of the new homiletic to have been heralded by a book written in 1971 by Fred Craddock called *As One Without Authority*.[9] Craddock challenged the habit of finding a single thought or idea in a Bible passage that could be argued out in a sermon. This he described as a 'packaged conclusion'.[10] Many preachers were actually trained to reduce a Scripture passage to three points (and these were usually itemized key words that started with the same letter). Preaching was related to the scientific preoccupation with logical proof. The role of preaching was thought to be to offer *answers*.

Craddock noticed that, in preparing the text to preach from, the preacher goes through a journey of experience. When preachers study Scripture, the text nearly always offers the thrill of a new discovery. Craddock's criticism of preaching was that preachers did not seem to be able to convey that thrill from the study to the pulpit for the congregation to share. Somewhere between the desk and the pulpit the experience went from the delight of treasure found to a dry essay. Craddock described his method of preaching as an inductive journey and so the preacher could be described as a travel courier helping the congregation on their journey.

The sermon as a journey is a powerful image. It was an idea that many other people developed. In one sentence Eugene Lowry has summarized the work of several of the principal writers whose models of preaching are evoked by powerful images and whose work has contributed forcefully to the new debate about homiletics:

> In metaphorical terms, we have not only [H. Grady] Davis's *tree* and Craddock's *trip*, but also R. E. C. Browne's *[poetic] gesture*, Tom Troeger's *music of speech*, David Buttrick's *move*, Henry Mitchell's *celebration*, Lucy Rose's *conversation*, David Schlafer's *play*, and Paul Scott Wilson's *spark of imagination* – as well as my *plot*, of course![11]

There is an impression of movement in all these images. What they all have in common is that they recognize preaching as a live and active event, not a static presentation. In the work of David Schlafer and Eugene Lowry in particular there is an emphasis on a plot, such as a story or a play might have. The sermon moves as a series of stages that begin by presenting a problem to explore. The problem keeps the listeners in suspense.

Eventually, the sermon does not end with a conclusion or an answer but with a *resolution*. The resolution comes about because the problem is held up to the good news of the Gospel. Such a sermon does not become 'closed down', indeed, it might conclude with a question rather than an answer. But what it will attempt to achieve is to send the congregation away with an idea or a problem to explore in their own minds.

This echoes very much the way Jesus himself preached. Take, for example, Luke 10.29-36 – the Parable of the Good Samaritan. Jesus tells a story that has suspense at its centre: Who will tend to the injured traveller? It closes with a delicious twist; the hero is a despised Samaritan, not a Jewish holy man. At the end of his narrative Jesus turns to his questioner and instead of closing with a concluding concrete statement he asks, 'Who do you think was this man's neighbour?'

If sermons do not lead to closed answers then religious mysteries can be explored without necessarily being proved. God is unknowable and this is recognized in the 'new homiletic'. If we are to know God in any way at all it is by offering experiences of God rather than discourses about God. This is summed up beautifully by someone who said that preachers have become used to giving the congregation a map to show them the way to the beach.

But the preacher's real task is to help the congregation to feel the wind in their hair and the spray of the sea on their cheeks.[12]

Preaching is no longer a dry, academic exercise. It has been rediscovered and is now an opportunity for creative and stimulating public speech, designed to offer the listeners a glimpse of the kingdom of God and their place in that kingdom.

Chapter 5

The role of the Reader in a collaborative Church

Caroline Pascoe

> This is the full meaning of collaborative ministry;
> not simply to renew the Church,
> but to enable the Church to be part of
> transforming the world.[1]

This chapter explores what it is to be a collaborative Church, the foundations and characteristics of collaborative ministry and, specifically, the role, opportunities and challenges of ministering as a Reader within a collaborative context.

Collaborative ministry takes many forms depending on where it develops and on the experience, age, gender, and theological awareness of the people involved. Its initial motivation might stem from need, from theological conviction, a desire to be fashionable or politically correct; from seeing collaboration at work and catching a vision; from reflecting on a good experience; from coming to realize that people really can achieve more and better together; from looking for ways of helping people take steps of faith; from knowing that each person is specially called and gifted by God; from noticing and encouraging gifts and ministries in others. There is no single model or blueprint, although there are characteristics (which this chapter explores) that distinguish it very clearly from 'helping the vicar' or delegation.

Collaborative ministry does not have to be difficult or expensive or involve grand schemes. For example, maintaining the list of those to pray for and visiting the sick and those in hospital has become a shared responsibility of a network of people across our benefice. In another benefice a Good Neighbour Group has been running for ten years offering care such as sitting with the lonely, sick or dying; collecting prescriptions; babysitting for single parents and much more. A member of a local ministry team was the inspiration, energy and practical impetus behind its beginning and now a small local coordinating group from the church and community runs it; through it an extraordinary range of gifts and ministries have found an opportunity for expression. In another parish a youth group session led by the Reader on 'listening to God' sparked the youth group into exploring local need and taking the initiative of cooking Christmas lunch at the church hall for anyone who was alone at Christmas. Collaborative ministry can flow from giving thoughtful attention to such basic starting points as: 'I can't cope with all the bereavement visiting on my own.' 'What do people think when the church is locked – can't we get a rota going?' 'Why does everything always get left to the vicar?' The question 'Why are there so few young families and so many divorces?' led in one parish to partnership between the council and the church to develop glebe land as low cost housing, a self-help parenting support group, as well as some soul searching as the parish reviewed its worship, witness and shared vision for the next five years.

A collaborative Christmas

For a number of years, Sheena, the Reader living in St Margaret's parish, has begun preparation for Christmas in September when the clergy, Readers and churchwardens meet to lay the foundations for the Advent and Christmas journey across the benefice. Together they review the life and witness of the local churches, local community needs and the current world context – and explore what is uppermost in local people's minds and concerns. This year, two of the Readers introduced a discussion on the particular significance of incarnation in this place at this time. Before their meeting a fortnight later they each prayed through the Principal Service readings for the Sundays of Advent and Christmas. They shared what they had heard and together identified the needs, opportunities and emphases to bring out in different ways in the different parishes of the benefice during Advent and Christmas.

Then, with one of the churchwardens, the organist, the Sunday school leader and village hall committee representative, Sheena issued an open invitation at St Margaret's to any others who felt particularly moved this year to share in preparing for Christmas in the parish. The other clergy, Readers and church-wardens did the same in the other parishes. At St Margaret's a group of eleven, including two teenagers, agreed to meet fortnightly. Between meetings group members prayed the readings and talked to local people. Through October Sheena led the group in reflection and study and they all shared responsibility for leading prayer. Then they moved to planning. Local people gave input on what had happened before and reflected on its strengths and weaknesses.

Together they talked about what they were hoping to achieve locally and across the benefice. They asked: 'What gifts and opportunities do we have?' 'What can we build on – like the carol service in the pub and the links the new headteacher is wanting to build between the church and primary school?' 'Who else do we need to talk to, consult, and work with?' When it came to designing the worship, Sheena and the Sunday school leader gave input as together they asked: 'How can we structure lively, accessible, prayerful services that enable all sorts and ages of people to worship?' – and much more.

Sometimes Sheena looks back wistfully to the days when she was able to plan one carol service that she would use at several churches. She remembers when she was able to choose her own favourite carols. Sometimes Paul, the vicar, wakes at three in the morning with a recurring nightmare about losing control. But Sheena knows she had never been so stretched theologically, educationally and liturgically in her ministry as a Reader until she began to resource others like this. Paul rejoices that his priestly ministry and special gift of healing has been released and drawn on as never before. As they reflect together about the long-term development of the benefice, the clergy, Readers and churchwardens rejoice in the growing confidence in each of the local Christian communities in taking responsibility for their worshipping and witnessing lives, for ministry and mission.

A shared vision for local ministry

At St John's the local ministry team and the PCC have spent nearly three years working with the local Community Trust to lay the foundations of a project to establish a drop-in centre and coffee bar in an empty shop on the local estate. Finally the centre staff team of three was put together. Mark, the Reader, was appointed to develop educational opportunities and church links; Dean was appointed as administrator and coordinator and Claire as community worker. Mark gave up his job as a primary school teacher to take part in the project; Claire had just taken early retirement as a social worker. Dean had sold his business in the previous year and was praying for an opportunity to use his administrative and financial gifts in God's service.

Members of the congregation and community staff the centre. The management group has an equal number of places for members of the Community Trust, the PCC and the local community. The project has been undergirded by prayer maintained by the Parish Prayer Link coordinated by May who has been housebound for many years and who was widowed two years ago. The group is linked by telephone and also through a weekly prayer sheet. Round the clock prayer began when May realized that shift workers and elderly who had trouble sleeping could have a ministry too – exercised at night.

Mark soon struggled with belonging to so many different groups – to the centre staff team as well as the PCC and local ministry team. They had to work through jealousy and suspicion at the closeness of the centre staff. There were tensions because the centre seemed to be attracting people away from the more traditional tasks of keeping church life going. It was necessary to let some activities die in order to free up time, gifts and energy. Mark found that his educational skills were needed as much among the congregation – as it struggled with the inevitable challenges of drugs on the premises, vandalism, homelessness – as they were in setting up open learning opportunities at the centre. But somehow it was the trust that had been built between people and the focus on prayer, which carried all that the centre was doing into the worshipping life of the congregation, that held it all together.

These two examples each illustrate Readers engaged in Reader ministry focused on 'preaching, teaching and leading worship ... in a pastoral context'.[2] However, they also paint pictures of Readers involved in and nurturing collaborative ministry in action.

Among other things, local Christians were:

- reflecting together on local need and doing that with local people;
- as churches and as individuals responding to God's particular call to them even when it was costly;
- taking decisions together and planning on the basis of shared vision;
- on journeys of personal and corporate faith development;
- ministering and being ministered to;
- worshipping together and being a worshipping, witnessing presence in their community;
- appreciating and drawing on God-given gifts in the local Christian and wider communities.

Between them the licensed ministers were:

- nurturing conditions where Christian community and collaborative ministry could flourish;
- checking that initiatives, preaching, teaching, community life were in line with their local church shared vision of God's call to them and drawing attention back to that vision where needed;
- exercising a ministry of oversight – discerning, praying, listening, encouraging, chastening;
- accompanying individuals and the community on journeys of faith;
- creating structures and opportunities to support new steps in faith and ministry.

In those examples as licensed lay ministers the Readers were:

- a constant reminder to the whole community that God calls all the baptized to discipleship and ministry in the whole of life;
- exercising a ministry of encouraging and resourcing theological reflection and enquiry;
- preaching, teaching and leading worship in such as way as to build up the gifts and ministries of others and to nurture the Christian communities on their journeys.

The roots of collaborative ministry

Collaborative ministry is increasingly seen as an authentically necessary expression of the Church's life. Readers, ordinands and other authorized ministers are increasingly trained to lead and to minister collaboratively and within collaborative contexts. But why?

The collaborative ministry illustrated in the examples above rests on a number of assumptions. The first is that God cares about the world he created and that as Church our primary responsibility is to work with him for the well-being and fulfilment of that world or, in other words, to collaborate with God in his mission. The second assumption is that God's call is equally inclusive of all the baptized people of God. The third is that licensed lay and ordained ministers have a particular leadership responsibility of encouraging and challenging individuals and society to be listening for, discerning and responding to God's call. In that spirit, the 2001 Church of England Report on Continuing Ministerial Education for lay and ordained ministers makes a core assertion that the Church needs ministers who 'stimulate and enable the whole church to participate more fully in the mission of God in the world'.[3]

Collaborative ministry is rooted in an understanding of Church in which the whole body of Christ is called to holiness, mission and ministry. All are responsible as active participants in Christ's mission and Christ's body. The point of being collaborative is not because it is fashionable or organizationally efficient; the point is that this is the abiding characteristic of Jesus' own ministry, and the community which he taught and empowered as his 'body'.

From its oldest roots our faith has taught that we are 'made in God's image' (Genesis 1.27). God calls us day by day to be shaped (and transformed) into that image (2 Corinthians 3.18), and with him to do his work in the world (John 17.18). To be and to do, shaped by God, is the root of being a collaborative Church and of collaborative ministry.

Concretely, what does this mean for local churches and for Readers? Among other things it means being careful that we really do follow through our Christian values and beliefs in how we behave individually and as Church and do not just delude ourselves. How we choose to shape ourselves as people and as Christian communities is vital, as is how we exercise Reader and any other authorized ministry. This starts with how we treat other people; how we take decisions (and who takes them); how we organize ourselves; how we understand and use power; how we communicate and share what we have.

Seeing 'how those Christians love one another' (see 1 John 3) could be part of inspiring this generation with a vision of a new world order – or it could confirm the widespread fear that any religion leads inevitably to division, injustice and hatred. In the Church of which we are a part, there are signs of growth and excitement but there is also pain, sadness and anger to the point that many feel they can no longer bear to belong. These are not abstract issues for academic theologians. They are what millions of teenagers are thinking about when they read Philip Pullman's Dark Materials Trilogy where two children grapple with a church that has disastrously lost its way, fight a cosmic battle between good and evil and choose how to play their part in building the 'republic of heaven'.[4] As Professor Daniel Hardy writes: 'if we are a "circle of God's life in the world", how do we restore that circle and make it a deepening spiral of participation in the life of God in the world? It is not too much to ask that we get our act together, and do the job properly!'[5] That is a shared responsibility for all Christians wherever they are. Being a collaborative Church is much more than sharing who leads the intercessions or working within a ministerial team: it is the Church's vocation. As Archbishop Rowan Williams puts it, vocation is 'what's left when all the games have stopped'.[6]

Such an enquiry into God and God's promises and unfolding desires and what is implied for the Church as the body of Christ is where a Reader's ministry begins; it is its focus, its guide, its root and what shapes its expression and outworking. For Readers, from such a basis flows a particular lay, preaching, teaching and liturgical ministry expressed within the pastoral context of the body of Christ called to share in God's mission in his world.

For these reasons the Report on Reader Ministry and Training places an emphasis on developing collaborative skills in Readers. The report is clear that:

> As well as working collaboratively with clergy and other ministers, Readers also need to work with and encourage other lay people both in the parish and in their place of work ... Readers have a special role in discerning and encouraging the ministerial gifts and skills of the congregation. The community of faith is thus enabled not only to

share in the mission of the Church but to make sense of the world at large and engage with it as part of their Christian discipleship ... Readers need to develop 'an ability to facilitate the learning and growth in faith of those to whom and with whom they minister.'[7]

The characteristics of collaborative ministry

Delegation or consultation is often mistaken for collaborative ministry. However, there are a number of distinctive marks or signs by which collaborative ministry can be recognized and which offer pointers for its further development.[8]

Quality of relationships – communion

Where the quality of the relationships is as important as the task in hand. Where attention is given to the form of church life as it is called to be shaped in the image of God. Where there is mutual accountability and responsibility for that life.

Partnership

Where people, gifts and ministries are valued and seen as complementary rather than in competition. Where the distinctive contribution of each person and each gift shines more clearly and is expressed more fully. Where the discovery of new gifts in the whole of life is seen as enriching the ministry of the body rather than detracting from church life.

Commitment to kingdom values

Where all share in a commitment to 'walking the talk' – to supporting each other in ministering, living and growing a community based on behaviour aligned with values 'made in the image of God'.

A company of people sharing a vision and on a journey

Where there is a shared vision of God's call to that community in that place at that time. Where the community travels light and structures and traditions are maintained for as long as they are positively contributing to the community response to God's call and mission in that place. Where there is a commitment to making the journey together – through the doubts, conflicts, uncertainties that will inevitably arise. Where decisions are taken together weighed against the shared vision and the shared values.

Sharing in God's mission

Where there is attentiveness to noticing where God is already active in the whole of life – and a commitment to supporting ministry in partnership with God wherever he is transforming the world. Where there is shared discernment of call and vision in the local church and all people are encouraged and supported in discerning and responding to God's particular call to them. Where the community chooses God's 'preferential option for the poor' and looks for opportunities to express 'venturesome love' wherever there is need.

The opportunities for exercising Reader ministry collaboratively

Given the above, the opportunities for Readers of exercising and nurturing collaborative ministry are huge. Many congregations are living the sort of theological journey I have been describing. Others are making the journey of discovery of the ministry and mission of the whole people of God driven by the painful realities of larger groupings of parishes and fewer clergy. Whatever the reason, Reader ministry, parish life and ecclesiology is changing. Increasingly congregations are discovering what it is to be 'ministering communities rather than communities gathered around a minister.'[9] Readers have a role as lay theological resourcers, as catalysts, enablers and reflectors, as 'Companions in Ministry and Mission', which is waiting to be developed: ministering *with* rather than *to*. As Kathy Galloway writes: 'It is in the "how" that theory becomes practice, intentions become actions, that we practise what we preach. "How" is where the word becomes flesh.'[10]

Readers will increasingly find themselves ministering within the context of ministry teams. These may be teams of clergy and Readers or local ministry teams of wider lay and ordained ministries. Whatever the make-up the team must be clear about its purpose and boundaries. For example: how a ministry team relates to and works with the PCC(s) so that, rather than usurping the leadership role of the PCC, it stimulates and deepens the quality of the leadership the PCC exercises. Similarly, it is easy for a ministry team to draw ministry to itself rather than enabling ministry throughout the parish. At its best a ministry team can be a catalyst for a parish journey of discovery so that attention is paid to the form of church life lived and to releasing ministry and mission involving many people.

Some Readers find the formation of a ministry team threatening to their ministry. In a collaborative Church a rich weave of gifts and ministries does typically develop over time. In such a complex context it is tempting to want to define what only a Reader can do – just as many wish it were possible to define what only a priest (a member of a local ministry team, a churchwarden, bishop or deacon) can do. But a collaborative Church is a reminder that each of those ministries is a part of an interconnected whole. The trick is to be clear about the particular focus, sign and reminder to the whole body that each ministry distinctively carries. Each makes its special contribution – a 'sign' of the emphases, roles and responsibilities necessary for the building up, chastening, ministry and mission of the whole body of Christ. That contribution can be as much through being as through doing. For example, how a Reader behaves within a team will be at least as powerful an influence on the tone and effectiveness of that team as any theoretical team-building insights that Reader might offer. As a lay person experienced in the joys and pain of ministry, a Reader can be an invaluable source of support and encouragement to others. All grow through learning together and new ministries develop.

However, the richest vein of opportunities for Readers to minister collabora-tively and be catalysts of collaborative ministry and mission comes not from finding new activities and tasks but in *how* they exercise their classically Reader ministry of preaching, teaching and leading worship in a pastoral context. For example:

Teaching

In a Church called to be collaborative, the Reader ministry of teaching offers an opportunity to foster learning environments where curiosity, exploration, puzzlement and wonder are normal and encouraged: 'I've never understood why ...' 'What would happen if ...?' 'At work when ...' 'What do you think when Jesus ...?' 'Wow – I've just had the most amazing experience ...' This requires Readers to understand and appreciate the different ways that people learn – so that worship, spirituality, discussion groups, sermons, activities are accessible by activists, reflectors, theorists, pragmatists alike. Readers can nurture a community journey of discovery where learning is with and from each other; where the insights, experience and puzzles of young and old, of people of all backgrounds are given equal attention and value.

Preaching

In a Church called to be collaborative, preaching is an opportunity to encourage chewing over and reflecting together on deep issues of life and faith – whether in church or in the sixth form common room or in the office. Readers have many opportunities to give focused attention to accompanying individuals and congregations over weeks and months as they ask questions, puzzle and grow. Ideas and insights, issues and dilemmas raised can be picked up and worked with; stories and experiences shared and reflected on together. Through disciplined prayer, biblical study and reflection with others, Readers can be part of exploring the challenge as well as the comfort of faith.

Leading worship

Leading worship offers endless opportunities over the long term for enabling each local Christian community to have the confidence and skills to express their lives and their love of God in worship in church, at home and in the whole of life. Readers will often also have the time and opportunities to collaborate in the creation of really apt liturgy enabling individuals and communities at significant times of life to worship in ways which celebrate, heal and transform.

Theological reflection

In a collaborative Church Readers have a vital ministry of developing the habit of viewing life through 'kingdom spectacles'. A Reader can help to nurture the habit of theological reflection so that, for example, the PCC naturally starts to ask: 'What might we be missing? Who else do we need to be listening to? Let's just stop and explore this further – What are the experiences of local people about this? What are the reasons behind what is happening? Let's pray, reflect and explore our shared vision before we decide how to respond.'

Pastoral context

Readers have the opportunity for long-term and in-depth work with the natural communities and networks of which they are a part. For example, in a collaborative Church the pastoral contexts in which a Reader is set offer opportunities for exploring with others what is maintaining the poverty, loneliness, ill health, and despair, anxiety you are noticing together. Together there is time to discern those issues that seem to be the particular local burden and to find ways of responding with more than temporary pastoral sticking plaster.

The challenges of ministering as a Reader within a Church called to be collaborative

The opportunities are endless and the call to be and to do shaped by God is clear; but choosing the collaborative route is not necessarily quick or easy.

The first steps in growing collaboration include encouraging people to think and to express their opinions and feelings. I remember being invited to lead an afternoon with a local Mothers' Union on how the Church and world are changing. I spoke a little and then I got them to begin to talk about their feelings, hopes and concerns. As a Reader who for them was a representative of the changing Church by which they felt so hurt, I left feeling shredded by the bitterness and anger that was expressed. But that meeting was the first step in a slow, painful and hopeful process of healing some deep, festering wounds locally which had to be attended to before trust could be rebuilt and any sense of shared purpose and responsibility in the Church explored.

I remember designing and introducing a new order of service for all-age worship of which I was very proud and then, some months later, inviting the congregation to stay behind for coffee to give me their feedback. Between them they were very gentle with me and in many ways very affirming, but by the end of the meeting I realized that I had unwittingly imposed something which they didn't really understand, didn't want and certainly weren't ready for. We agreed to meet again to explore what would help us to reach local families and together express our worship as a church on a journey. We have ended up with something far more creative than I could have imagined or thought possible.

Working closely with a good friend who is also a Reader I was involved in a project for which letters needed to be sent out. My friend prepared the letter. I saw it waiting for copying and, as a perfectionist, made some changes and then sent it. I was shocked to discover later how deeply undermined she felt by what I had done. I still think back with pain at the anger, misunderstanding and hurt to which that small incident gave rise. I blush at my ineptitude. We needed to draw on deep reserves of prayer, forgiveness, love and understanding in order not to end up with a running sore or a rift between us.

It is exciting to imagine ministry and church life and mission based on principles of mutuality, flourishing, gifts, etc., where together you achieve more than you ever could alone, but the reality is that it takes perseverance, forgiveness, patience, love, understanding, mutual respect, and the grace of the Holy Spirit for this to be remotely possible.

A Reader will have many opportunities for ministering collaboratively and nurturing collaboration. But not everything that appears to be collaborative is truly so or has the result of building up the body of Christ to share in God's mission. Often what appears to be collaboration is really delegation, selling or consultation. It is not even delegation when you pass a reading across at the last minute. It is delegation when you give a responsibility and take it back when you don't like what has been done or decide that now you would prefer to make other arrangements. It is selling when you have a plan about which you want to convince others. It is consultation when you want to hear what they think but you will go away and decide. The degree to which others will own, implement and put their energy behind a decision is the degree to which they have been involved in taking it.

Many Readers and clergy were selected for a self-starting individual ministry with role models that prized self-sacrifice and leading from the front. There are many stories of Readers who are deeply hurt because their ministry is not being encouraged and used by clergy. There are many stories of lay people who are deeply hurt because their ministry is not being encouraged and used by Readers. There are many stories of licensed ministers who have been burnt out by the demands and expectations placed upon them by lay people. It is a mutual responsibility for all Christians regularly to ask themselves, alone and with a spiritual director or friend: How am I supporting the growth and flourishing of ...? How am I discerning and nurturing the ministry of ...? In what ways am I contributing to building up the body of Christ here, to God's mission in his world? – and then to be prepared to start again, forgiving and being forgiven.

What is needed to foster collaborative ministry?

As a Reader don't expect to introduce collaboration overnight or on your own. Attempting to move from delegation to collaboration in one leap is a sure source of confusion, pain and disillusionment. Growing a collaborative Church and collaborative ministry is a long-term project of developing shared vision and growing trust and honesty.

Start small. Work, for example, on how you relate to other authorized ministers – collaboration needs leaders who have experienced the joys and pains of collaboration for themselves and can therefore consciously work to foster the conditions for collaboration to flourish. A vicar or Reader who leads by sarcasm and put-downs will never grow an environment where people know they are valued, respected, and are safe enough to take risks of faith and growth. Some deep and painful personal change may be necessary.

As you preach, teach and lead worship take care to contribute to the development of a shared vision of God's call to your local church at this time and in this place. Encourage your congregations really to get to know and to serve the particular communities and the networks of which they are part. Take time to find out the cares, concerns, needs, and joys of local people.

Encourage everyone to take personal responsibility starting with what they say: 'I feel ...', 'I think ...', rather than 'everyone knows that no one likes ...'.

Regularly review progress against the marks of collaborative ministry. As a Reader, conduct at least an annual review of your ministry – preferably with a spiritual director or soul friend – or with one or two local people you trust to be sensitively honest with you. Do the same with the PCC, at a parish away day, with each congregation and with other ministers. Against the marks ask:

> What is going well?
> What are the sticking points or difficulties we are encountering?
> What insights can we build on for the future?

What a collaborative Church particularly needs of Readers today

Sheena commented that she had never been so stretched theologically, educationally and liturgically in her ministry as Reader until she began to resource others and minister collaboratively with them. My own ministry has never been so fulfilling as well as so demanding as when I have been working collaboratively and consciously looking to encourage and enable the whole body of Christ.

The following skills, attributes and commitments are important in Readers with a collaborative ministry:

- a continuing commitment to developing your own skills and resources as a Reader through prayer, study, experience of and theological reflection on the breadth of life today;
- a commitment to nurturing Christian communities on journeys of faith, and in their listening to God;
- a passion to see others flourish and grow;
- a willingness to let go of your own pet projects and plans and to encourage others;
- resilience and perseverance;
- knowing that collaboration requires forgiveness and being forgiven – regularly;
- a mature awareness of your own gifts and weaknesses – and of your impact on others;
- valuing and keeping your eyes open for the particular contribution you can make as a Reader to the life and witness of your local Christian communities;
- generosity about the gifts and ministries of others; curiosity, flexibility and openness;
- knowing that your lay ministry has dignity as one of the baptized and is not second best;
- 'walking the talk' yourself – modelling the behaviours needed to build trust and collaboration;
- being prepared to learn from anyone and anywhere, always;
- paying attention to where God is already at work.

In the end though, what it all comes down to is very simple. As Bishop Stewart Zabriskie of Nevada put it at a meeting on collaborative ministry and mission at the 1998 Lambeth Conference:

> The first and most basic commitment we have as partners in ministry development is to listen to and pray for the Holy Spirit's guidance.

Remember who is in charge of this church. This brings us right up against the greatest obstacle, our need to be in control. For us, and we really have to work on this, to listen is a kind of 'prayer without ceasing' maintaining the beginner's mind, ready to accept gifts of imagination or energy and a sense of humour which amounts to not taking ourselves more seriously than we take God.[11]

As such a Reader, ministering collaboratively with Christian communities on a journey, you will never run out of opportunities to minister and be ministered to, to lead, nurture, encourage, wonder, grow and learn wherever you are.

Chapter 6

Selection and training for Reader ministry

Wendy Thorpe

Selection

Introduction

Now you have some idea of what being a Reader is all about, you may feel that God is calling you to this ministry. Or perhaps, the idea was not yours. You have been approached by your incumbent or by friends who have perceived in you the qualities needed for a leadership role in the Church. You may feel receptive to their suggestions or uncertain. What should you do next?

The selection process is designed to test your vocation and to discern whether you have the maturity of faith, the personality and character and the potential for training which a Reader candidate requires. The selection process can take up to six months, sometimes longer. This length of time has many advantages. It gives you time to reflect and pray about your vocation and to consider what changes will be necessary in your life, if you are selected. It also gives you time to discuss the possible implications with your family and colleagues. Time can be profitably spent talking to other Readers in your diocese about their work, and reading whatever you can about Reader ministry.

Before you even begin the selection process it is important to consider other possibilities for ministry. All dioceses have vocations officers who can be contacted for advice and help. You should ask about other types of lay authorized ministry in the diocese and also consider whether God might be calling you to an ordained ministry that is either full-time and paid or part-time and voluntary. Read everything you can about these different types of ministry. Your vocations officer will be able to suggest suitable titles and may have special leaflets on ministry opportunities in your diocese. Time spent at this stage will help you to be confident about your decision to go forward as a Reader or it will open up other possibilities for you to explore.

Whatever ministry you hope to be selected for, the House of Bishops' policy on Child Protection requires ministerial candidates to complete a confidential statement. This can be obtained from your diocesan officer. When completed, the diocese will arrange for it to be checked against the Index of the Department of Health Consultancy Service which is a service for checking the suitability of candidates for appointments to posts which may involve unsupervised contact with children.

Nomination for selection

However your sense of vocation to Reader ministry develops, other people are also involved in its discernment. You may have spoken already to your incumbent, members of the parish ministry team, other Readers and the Warden of Readers, but the clear support of your local church must be obtained.

The first step is for your incumbent or priest-in-charge and your Parochial Church Council, acting together, to nominate you for training as a Reader. It should be possible, at this time, to explore a potential role for you, whether in your own parish, another parish or in the wider Church. A well-staffed parish may be able and willing to support your training even if your ministry will be elsewhere, for example, in a local hospital, a prison, or a parish nearby that needs help.

The PCC should approve a statement about this possible role for you to indicate its commitment to supporting you during training. The statement should go with the preliminary paperwork to the Warden of Readers. The paperwork will include an official form supplying your personal details, the names and addresses of two referees of whom one at least should know you in the context of life outside the church, and a letter of written support from your priest.

The selection conference

Before too long you should receive from the warden of Readers, or the person delegated in your diocese to run selection conferences for Reader candidates, a letter giving you details of where and when you will be interviewed. Selection conferences are usually held two or three times per year, often in the autumn, spring and early summer, for up to eight candidates at a time.

Dioceses vary in the way they manage selection but most will expect you to attend for a whole day. During the day, you will be interviewed by at least three different people. After the interviews, they will meet to share their insights and perceptions and to decide whether to recommend you for training.

Careful consideration is given to the recommendations of your priest and referees.

You may also be asked to give a short talk to discern whether you have potential skills as a communicator and to see whether you find it easy and natural to talk about your faith. You might also be given a practical task such as responding to a difficult pastoral problem or leading a group discussion.

However nervous you may feel beforehand, most candidates agree that the day is stimulating and helpful. The selectors have your best interests in mind. If you are not suitable for Reader ministry, it is better to find out at the beginning of the process rather than to undergo a long training and discover it later. If the training is discerned to be too difficult given your present commitments, again, it is better to know straight away, rather than struggle on and have to withdraw later.

As soon as possible after the interviews you will hear the decision of the panel of selectors. These decisions often have to receive the approval of the bishop before they are released. If the bishop is away or extremely busy, delays may be inevitable.

If you are selected, it is for Reader *training*, not for admission as a Reader at some future date. That decision is made at the end of your training in consultation with your incumbent, your training officer, the bishop and the warden of Readers.

If you are not selected for training, the reasons will be shared with you and your incumbent. Normally you will be able to talk over the situation with the warden of Readers or someone delegated for the purpose who will give you help and guidance.

It is possible you will be asked to re-apply at a future date. This may be because you are perceived to have potential but lack maturity in your faith or practical experience of ministry in your parish, or other similar reasons.

Criteria for selection

What sort of people are the selectors looking for? The House of Bishops has advised dioceses that they should look for the following qualities, characteristics and potential in Reader candidates.

Ministry in the Church of England:
You must be baptized and episcopally confirmed and a regular communicant of the Church of England, familiar with its traditions and practices.

Vocation:
You should be able to talk about your sense of vocation to ministry, both your own conviction and the extent to which others have confirmed it.

Faith:
You will need to show a basic understanding of the Christian faith and a desire to deepen that understanding, a personal commitment to Christ and a capacity to communicate the gospel.

Spirituality:
Your spiritual discipline of prayer, Bible study and regular worship should underpin, energize and sustain your daily life.

Personality and character:
You should be a person of integrity with sufficient maturity and stability to show that you can sustain the demanding role of a minister and cope with change and pressure in a flexible and balanced way.

Relationships:
You need to be self-aware and self-accepting as a basis for open and healthy personal and pastoral relationships. You will need to show your ability and willingness to cooperate with others sometimes as a leader or sometimes as a team member.

Potential for training:
You must be capable of undertaking a rigorous course of study and ministerial preparation in your spare time. You will need an open and enquiring mind.

Fortunately, no one is expected to score full marks on these criteria. You are not expected to be the archangel Gabriel! However, the role of a Reader today is wide and demanding. It is right for the Church to be rigorous in its selection.

After selection and before training

This is a most valuable time. It is important not to waste it. It is an opportunity to prepare yourself and those close to you before training begins.

As soon as you hear that you have been selected, it is a good idea to ask for an appointment with your incumbent to talk over your present role in the parish. You may be involved in numerous activities. It is vital that most of these are passed to others before your training begins in order to get the most from your training. Give up roles such as church treasurer, churchwarden, organist, choir mistress, and Sunday school leader. No one is indispensable. But keep, in moderation, activities like reading in church, leading prayers, planning informal services, preaching, teaching or pastoral work. These will all give you valuable experience for the future.

What about your family? In an age where family life is under threat and marriages frequently disintegrate, it is important to talk to your spouse and children about your future commitments and what effect this will have on them. When you plan the allocation of your time, it is essential to give them quality time, too. They may have suggestions and ideas about how you can achieve this.

If you have a full-time job, whether paid or voluntary, now is the time to consult with your employer and colleagues. Can occasional days off for training be negotiated? Can you work flexi-hours? Can you complete a difficult or time-consuming piece of work for your employer before you start training in order to lighten your workload later? There is much to think about and discuss. Employers can be extremely generous and helpful if given plenty of warning about your plans.

If time off is not an issue for you, why not get down to some pre-course reading? Once you start your course, time will be at a premium and there will never be enough time to read all the books recommended. Consult the director of Reader training in your diocese and ask for a book list.

Training

Introduction

Once selected, you will be eager to know about your training. Training is provided by your diocese. There are 44 dioceses in the Church of England and almost as many training schemes. This is intentional and has many advantages. Usually, diocesan schemes can reflect local circumstances far better than a centralized training scheme. They are also more flexible, more imaginative and more readily able to adapt to changing needs and circumstances. However, Reader ministry is nationally authorized and accredited, so every diocesan scheme is expected to meet national criteria and is regularly moderated to ensure this. This means that, in practice, there is considerable similarity between the diocesan schemes. It is therefore possible to describe what your training will consist of, with the proviso that the practice in your diocese might vary in some respects.

Training for life

The most important concept to grasp is that Reader training is not for a fixed period of time. Once selected, and later admitted to Reader ministry, you are committing yourself to a lifetime of training; training in the widest sense which will certainly include reading, Bible study, watching certain TV programmes, exploring the Internet, as well as workshops, courses, retreats and conferences. This commitment is essential because of the pace of change in society and the Church, and in Reader ministry itself. If you are to keep abreast of all these changes and have a ministry that is well-informed and relevant, it is essential that you take seriously the concept of lifelong training. It begins after selection. It continues with initial training, followed by post-admission training, and then continuing ministerial education.

Readers who work in occupations outside the Church will not find this concept difficult to understand or accept. Most employers today expect employees to undertake regular in-service training. Today's Readers pride themselves on a professional approach to their ministry, a professionalism which includes a strong expectation and commitment to training.

Preparing for study

Many Reader candidates have degrees but it may be a number of years since they were at university and their study skills are often rusty. Others, particularly older Reader candidates who were educated at a time when university education was for the very few, may never have developed study skills such as speed reading and taking notes, nor the ability to write essays.

Some dioceses now provide 'Return to study' courses or 'Study skills' workshops, but if not, it is worth enquiring about local adult education courses. Most Further Education centres provide short courses of this sort and there are grants if you are on a low income.

Initial training

Most initial training schemes last three years. Tuition is provided free for Reader trainees, although you will be expected to cover the cost of your travel to tutorials and residential weekends and to provide your own books. Parishes often assist with these expenses and diocesan grants are available for those on a low income. The number of hours you need to allocate each week will vary greatly according to your academic ability, knowledge, skills, experience, and speed of working. Your director of training will be able to give you a rough idea, but you should allow a minimum of six to eight hours per week to prepare for and attend tutorials, and for reading. Terms are normally eight to ten weeks in length, leaving you with about twenty-two weeks in the year for written work, projects and practical ministry in your parish.

Trainees vary in the amount of time they have available for study. Those who are retired or work part-time may have little difficulty, but if you are in a busy full-time job or caring for children, elderly parents or handicapped members of the family, you may find the pressures of study daunting. This is why it is recommended that you give up commitments in your parish during your initial training unless they directly help you in that training.

If you do get overwhelmed, see your director of training or tutor. Most courses are flexible enabling you to take time off and repeat the unit later or to take longer to complete your study, perhaps four years instead of three. But most trainees find that, after the initial shock of returning to study, they settle into a sensible and practical routine without undue stress on themselves or their families.

If, when you look at the syllabus, you think you may be repeating work covered in the last five years, you can ask for some exemption. Dioceses vary in their approach to this but it is always well worth talking with the director of training if you feel you have a strong case and can provide evidence. This is called accredited prior learning (APL).

Your initial training will be rigorous. Much will be expected of you and asked of you. But you have an exciting three years ahead. You will make new and lasting friendships. You will be challenged mentally and spiritually. You will acquire knowledge, new skills and the confidence to begin your Reader ministry.

A grounding in theology

Readers are called primarily to a preaching and teaching ministry in the Church. Many Readers are also able to bring theological resources to people in the community where they live and work. Therefore it is essential for you to acquire a thorough grounding in theology.

You will study the Old and New Testaments and explore the methods and insights of biblical criticism and interpretation. Church history will be important so that you can understand how divergent traditions and doctrines have occurred. You will also explore the diversity of traditions within the Church of England and their significance for the contemporary Church. You will look at traditional and contemporary expressions of spirituality. You will study the theology of worship, the place of liturgy in the Church of England, and its significance for the development and practice of public worship. You will encounter, and reflect upon, a variety of models of mission. You will look at contemporary theological and ethical issues. You will examine what it means to be a disciple within the community of the Church and the wider world.

The usual pattern is for you to meet weekly or fortnightly with other trainees and your tutor, either on a Saturday or Sunday or on a weekday evening. There will be an opportunity to worship together, to learn and to discuss. For trainees unable to get to a local centre, there may be distance learning material provided. But most trainees find that the stimulation and support of group colleagues is one of the most important and enjoyable parts of training.

Part of your training in theology will be practical. You may be involved in group projects, for example, exploring the history of a local church or working out a creed for the twenty-first century. Most dioceses arrange for trainees to have a short placement in a nearby parish as different as possible from your own. You will probably be asked to keep a diary about this experience and reflect on what you see and hear.

Skills

In addition to your training in theology you will be expected to acquire the skills needed to preach, teach, lead services and have a pastoral and leadership role in your parish. You will normally receive some diocesan teaching before putting these skills gradually into practice in your parish under the general supervision of your incumbent.

Preaching

Readers are the Church of England's lay preachers. They may be asked to preach in many different types of church and at a variety of services. The development of skills in preaching should be lifelong for Readers, and training begins as early as possible. Not only will you learn the craft of sermon construction and effective delivery, but also how to use commentaries and other tools in order to set Bible passages and stories in their wider contexts and handle passages and themes appropriately and imaginatively.

As important as preaching in church is the ability to communicate the gospel in informal situations like family services and services at old people's homes. Sharing the good news at work, in the market place and at the school gates is another vital skill in a society which is no longer predominantly Christian and which puts a high value on informality.

Teaching

Most Readers will be involved in some form of adult teaching or training, so a good basic grounding in adult learning theory as well as practice in the many necessary skills is important. Many trainee Readers are schoolteachers professionally. But teaching children and young people requires different skills and schoolteachers do not usually make the best teachers of adults, unless they receive additional training.

As a Reader you will be called on for a wide variety of work. You may be asked to lead house groups, healing prayer groups or Alpha groups. Or you may be responsible for adult confirmation classes, baptism preparation or marriage preparation. Perhaps you will have a training role either in the parish, helping lay people to lead intercessions and read at services, or perhaps in the diocese helping with Reader training, and diocesan Bible study courses. Reader trainees learn, among other things, how to create good learning environments for adults and how to choose varied and appropriate teaching methods. Other skills you will need to learn include leading group discussions and understanding how groups work.

Leading worship

Readers have an important liturgical role in the Church of England. You will learn how to lead a variety of services in many different types of Anglican churches, not just your own. These will include Morning and Evening Prayer, the Ministry of the Word in the Eucharist, funeral services and informal services like all-age worship. You will also learn about assisting with the administration of bread and wine, helping at baptisms especially if you have been involved in preparing parents and godparents, and leading Extended Communion. You will be trained to use your voice effectively for singing and speaking. You will learn how to get the best from sound systems. And you will be encouraged to be imaginative and creative in devising informal services.

Pastoral work

Readers have a pastoral ministry both in their parishes and where they work and live. Those who take funerals regularly are greatly involved in bereavement counselling and follow-up visits, while those who administer home communion visit the sick, the elderly and the housebound. In hospitals, hospices and prisons, Readers minister to the sick, the lonely and the distressed.

In many dioceses now there are lay ministers authorized to specialize in pastoral ministry. They may be called 'lay pastoral assistants' or 'pastoral workers', or something similar. In these dioceses your pastoral role will be more focused and grounded in your teaching, preaching and liturgical role, but it will still be significant as it is impossible to separate the roles completely.

Training for pastoral work focuses on listening skills, sharing faith in one-to-one situations, praying for people in informal settings and understanding bereavement. Workshops and short courses are useful but you will find that shadowing someone skilled in pastoral work in your parish is often the best training. Some courses require you to do a compulsory pastoral project as part of your initial training.

Spirituality

During training, you will be encouraged to develop a discipline of prayer, worship and Bible study to resource you for the demands of your ministry. You may be asked to find a spiritual director or soul friend to guide you during training and afterwards. Most dioceses keep lists of suitable people for you to approach but your incumbent or tutor, because they know you well, can best help you to find the person who will be right for you.

The Church provides many opportunities for spiritual growth and your spiritual director can advise you. Most dioceses have retreat houses with varied programmes and organize pilgrimages to centres of spirituality at home and abroad.

There will be opportunities during your training to share worship with trainees in your group. Some will be from different spiritual traditions to your own. This can be a rich opportunity for developing and extending your own spirituality.

Leadership

Readers, because of their theological and practical training and their visible role in worship, are regarded as important members of their church leadership teams. As lay leaders they have a vital role in encouraging and enabling the congregation to fulfil their own individual ministries in the Church and in the wider world.

Training for this role varies considerably from diocese to diocese but all take seriously the need for Readers to be flexible and collaborative in their style of working. Training teams, made up of clergy and Readers working together, model good practice. Day workshops on collaborative working, group dynamics and enabling the ministry of others are becoming more usual, although more often found in post-admission training rather than initial training.

Post-admission training

When you have finished your three-year initial training to the satisfaction of all concerned, you will be admitted as a Reader at a special annual service at your diocesan cathedral. You will also be licensed to a particular parish or group of parishes, or to a sector ministry such as a hospital or prison.

Admission is not a mark of omnicompetence. It is a public acknowledgement that you now have a basic grounding in knowledge and skills and that you are ready to begin putting your knowledge and skills into practice as a lay minister rather than as a trainee.

If your training has been effective you will be confident about beginning your ministry, but you will also be aware of how much more you have to learn. You will be keen to go on learning and you will be able to take responsibility for your own future learning.

Of course, you will experience enormous relief at having survived three years of rigorous training and will want to take a break. A holiday is a good idea before you plunge into the demands of Reader ministry.

Your ministry, however, will soon reveal to you gaps in your knowledge and skills training. Post-admission training is designed to help. Increasing numbers of dioceses are now making this available to Readers. Some dioceses, in order not to overwhelm Reader trainees in their initial training, leave important topics to post-admission training. For example, many dioceses leave funeral training or training for teaching to this post-admission period.

CME

These letters stand for Continuing Ministerial Education. Your diocese will have a CME officer and a CME budget, either to provide direct funding for courses you may want to undertake as part of your in-service training or for the provision of diocesan courses usually open to all ministers, lay and ordained.

Because of the importance of continuing education for ministers, many Readers' boards are now considering appointing their own CME officers for Readers to ensure that Readers have access to the continuing training and funding they need.

Conclusion

All this can sound rather daunting for a ministry which is part-time and unpaid. You may be asking yourself; 'Will I cope? Will I manage to fit all this training into my busy life?'

About five hundred Readers are admitted every year. They come from all walks of life and educational background, from manual workers to university professors. Be assured, it is possible and will be a source of great joy and satisfaction. If God has called you to be a Reader, you can be confident that he will enable you to find the time and the energy and the commitment to make proper preparation.

Appendix

The Canons

E 4   Of Readers

1. A lay person, whether man or woman, who is baptized and confirmed and who satisfies the bishop that he is a regular communicant of the Church of England may be admitted by the bishop of the diocese to the office of Reader in the Church and licensed by him to perform the duties which may lawfully be performed by a Reader according to the provisions of paragraph 2 of this Canon or which may from time to time be so determined by Act of Synod.

2. It shall be lawful for a Reader:

   (a) to visit the sick, to read and pray with them, to teach in Sunday school and elsewhere, and generally to undertake such pastoral and educational work and to give such assistance to any minister as the bishop may direct;

   (b) during the time of divine service to read Morning and Evening Prayer (save for the Absolution), to publish banns of marriage at Morning and Evening Prayer (on occasions on which a layman is permitted by statute law so to do, and in accordance with the requirements of that law), to read the word of God, to preach, to catechize the children, and to receive and present the offerings of the people;

   (c) to distribute the holy sacrament of the Lord's Supper to the people.

2A. The bishop may also authorize a Reader to bury the dead or to read the burial service before, at or after a cremation but only, in each case, with the goodwill of the persons responsible and at the invitation of the minister of a parish or an extra-parochial place within the meaning of section 1 of the Deaconesses and Lay Ministry Measure 1972.

When a cure is vacant the reference in this paragraph to the minister of a parish shall be construed as a reference to the rural dean.

3. The bishop of every diocese shall keep a register book wherein shall be entered the names of every person whom he has either admitted to the office of Reader or licensed to exercise that office in any place.

E 5   Of the nomination and admission of Readers

1. A candidate for the office of Reader in a parish or district shall be nominated to the bishop by the minister of that parish or district; and a candidate for the said office in a wider area by one of the rural deans or archdeacons after consultation with the minister of his parish or district.

2. The nominator in making such a nomination shall also satisfy the bishop that the said person is of good life, sound in faith, a regular communicant, and well fitted for the work of a Reader, and provide all such other information about the said person and the duties which it is desired that he should perform as the bishop may require.

3. No person shall be admitted to the office of Reader in the Church except it be found on examination, held by the bishop or by competent persons appointed by the bishop for this purpose, that he possesses a sufficient knowledge of Holy Scripture and of the doctrine and worship of the Church of England as set forth in *The Book of Common Prayer*, that he is able to read the services of the Church plainly, distinctly, audibly, and reverently, and that he is capable both of teaching and preaching.

4. Every person who is to be admitted to the office of Reader shall first, in the presence of the bishop by whom he is to be so admitted or of the bishop's commissary, make the declarations set out below, the preface which precedes the Declaration of Assent in paragraph 1(1) of Canon C15 (with the appropriate adaptations) having first been spoken by the bishop or commissary:

> I, A, B, do so affirm, and accordingly declare my belief in the Faith which is revealed in the Holy Scriptures and set forth in the catholic creeds and to which the historic formularies of the Church of England bear witness; and in public prayer I will use only the forms of service which are authorized or allowed by Canon.

> I, A, B, will give due obedience to the Lord Bishop of C and his successors in all things lawful and honest.

5. The bishop shall admit a person to the office of Reader by the delivery of the New Testament, but without imposition of hands.

6. The bishop shall give to the newly admitted reader a certificate of his admission to the office; and the admission shall not be repeated if the Reader shall move to another diocese.

E 6   Of the licensing of Readers

1. No person who has been admitted to the office of Reader shall exercise his office in any diocese until he has been licensed so to do by the bishop thereof:

Provided that, when any Reader is to exercise his office temporarily in any diocese, the written permission of the bishop shall suffice.

1A. A licence authorizing a Reader to serve in a benefice in respect of which a team ministry is established may be in a form which specifies the term of years for which the licence shall have effect.

2. Every Reader who is to be licensed to exercise his office in any diocese shall first, in the presence of the bishop by whom he is to be licensed, or of the commissary of such bishop, (a) make the declarations of assent and of obedience in the form and manner prescribed by paragraph 4 of Canon E 5; (b) make and subscribe the declaration following:

> I, A, B, about to be licensed to exercise the office of Reader in the parish (or diocese) of C, do hereby promise to endeavour, as far as in me lies, to promote peace and unity, and to conduct myself as becomes a worker for Christ, for the good of his Church, and for the spiritual welfare of [my]* all people. I will give due obedience to the Bishop of C and his successors and the minister in whose cure I may serve, in all things lawful and honest.

If the declarations of assent and of obedience have been made on the same occasion in pursuance of paragraph 4 of Canon E5 it shall not be necessary to repeat them in pursuance of this paragraph and in the declaration set out above the words 'the Bishop of C and his successors' and may be omitted.

3. The bishop of a diocese may by notice in writing revoke summarily, and without further process, any licence granted to a Reader within his diocese for any cause which appears to him to be good and reasonable, after having given the Reader sufficient opportunity of showing reason to the contrary; and the notice shall notify the Reader that he may, within 28 days from the due date on which he receives the notice, appeal to the archbishop of the province in which that diocese is situated.

On such an appeal the archbishop may either hear the appeal himself or appoint a person holding the office of diocesan bishop or suffragan bishop in his province (otherwise than in the diocese concerned) to hear the appeal in his place; and, after hearing the appeal or, if he has appointed a bishop to hear the appeal in his place, after receiving a report in writing from that bishop, the archbishop may confirm, vary or cancel the revocation of the licence as he considers just and proper, and there shall be no appeal from the decision of the archbishop.

Where the see of the archbishop is vacant or the archbishop is also the bishop of the diocese concerned, any reference in the preceding provisions of this paragraph to the archbishop of the province shall be construed as a reference to the archbishop of the other province, but any bishop appointed by the archbishop of the other province by virtue of this paragraph shall be a bishop serving in the province which contains the diocese concerned.

Any appeal under this paragraph shall be conducted in accordance with rules approved by the Archbishops of Canterbury and York; and any such rules may provide for the appointment of one or more persons to advise the archbishop or bishop hearing such an appeal or any question of law arising in the course thereof.

3A. Where a bishop has granted a licence to a Reader to serve in his diocese for a term of years specified in the licence, the bishop may revoke that licence under paragraph 3 of this Canon before the expiration of that term, and where he does so that Reader shall have the like right of appeal as any other Reader whose licence is revoked under that paragraph.

4. No bishop shall license any Reader to be a stipendiary in any place until he has satisfied himself that adequate provision has been made for the stipend of the said Reader, for his insurance against sickness or accident, and for a pension on his retirement.

Note: *The word 'my' should have been removed by Amending Canon No. 23. A future Amending Canon will correct this omission, But in the meantime, the word should be omitted as required by the sense.*

Notes

Chapter 1

1. *Working as One Body*, Church House Publishing, 1995.

Chapter 3

1. There is more discussion of the Christian work ethic, and of the implications of new technology, in the report of the Churches' Enquiry into Unemployment and the Future of Work (CCBI, 1997) of which the present author was executive secretary.
2. Material for services on this Sunday is provided each year by Church Action on Poverty, Central Buildings, Oldham Street, Manchester, M1 1JT.

Chapter 4

1. Michael Harry Cranston, 'Reader Ministry in the Church of England', Dissertation for MA in Religious Studies, Chichester: University College, 1999, p. 58; Carolyn Headley, *Readers and Worship in the Church of England*, Grove Books Ltd, 2000, p. 10.
2. Robin Gill, *A Vision for Growth*, SPCK, 1993, p. 77.
3. David Schlafer, *Your Way with God's Word*, Cowley Publications, 1995, p. xi.
4. David Day, *A Preaching Workbook*, Lynx, 1998, p. 117.
5. Day, *A Preaching Workbook*, p. 32.
6. David Schlafer, *Surviving the Sermon*, Cowley Publications, 1992.
7. Day, *A Preaching Workbook*, p. 132.
8. A good introduction to 'the new homiletic' can be found in the first chapter of: Eugene Lowry, *The Sermon: Dancing the Edge of Mystery*, Abingdon Press, 1997.
9. Fred Craddock, *As One Without Authority*, Phillips University, 1974.
10. Craddock, *As One Without Authority*, p. 67.
11. Lowry, *The Sermon*, p. 15. The works referred to in the quotation are: H. Grady Davis, *Design for Preaching*, Fortress Press, 1959; R. E. C. Browne, *The Ministry of the Word*, Fortress Press, 1959; Thomas Troeger, *Imagining the Sermon*, Abingdon Press, 1990; David Buttrick, *Homiletic*, SCM Press, 1987; Henry Mitchell, *The Recovery of Preaching*, Harper & Row, 1977; Lucy Rose, 'Preaching in the Round Table Church', PhD dissertation, Graduate School of Emory University, 1994; David Schlafer, *Surviving the Sermon*, Cowley Publications, 1992; Paul Scott Wilson, *The Practice of Preaching*, Abingdon Press, 1995; Eugene Lowry, *The Homiletical Plot*, John Knox Press, 1975.
12. Reference unknown.

Chapter 5

1. *The Sign We Give* – Report from the Working Party on Collaborative Ministry, Bishops' Conference of England and Wales, Matthew James Publishing, 1995, p. 13.
2. *Reader Ministry and Training: 2000 and Beyond*, Ministry Division, 2000, p. 29.
3. *Mind The Gap*, Church House Publishing, 2001, p. 33, para. 3.24.
4. Philip Pullman, *The Amber Spyglass*, Scholastic Press, 2000.
5. D. Hardy, *God's Ways with the World*, T&T Clark, 1996, p. 222.
6. Rowan Williams, *Open to Judgement*, quoted in Francis Dewar, *Invitations: God's Calling for Everyone*, SPCK, 1996.
7. *Reader Ministry and Training*, p. 31, para. 5.23.
8. The ideas for these categories have been developed from *The Sign We Give*.
9. Wesley Frensdorff in J. Borgeson and L. Wilson (eds), *Reshaping Ministry*, Jethro Publications, 1990, p. 4.
10. Kathy Galloway, *Starting Where We Are: The Story of a Neighbourhood Project*, Wild Goose Publications, 1998, p. 12.
11. Bishop Stewart Zabriskie of Nevada, USA in a presentation given at the 1998 Lambeth Conference meeting on 'Local Ministry and the Future Shape of the Church's Mission' hosted by the Edward King Institute for Ministry Development.

Further reading on general Ministry issues

Gordon Kuhrt, *An Introduction to Christian Ministry*, Church House Publishing, 2000
Gordon Kuhrt, *Ministry Issues for the Church of England*, Church House Publishing, 2001

These books provide a wider theological background and context. The second book contains two chapters specifically on Reader Ministry.

Index